PRAISE FOR *THE PROFITABLE SPIRITUAL MEDIUM*

The Profitable Spiritual Medium gave me the exact roadmap to expand my business and craft offers that resonate. Melissa's blend of spirit wisdom and business savvy impressively turned my business from ok to $$$ in just a few months.

—**Emily Snyder,** Intuitive Psychic Medium, Connected Intuition

For too long, spiritual gifts came with a vow of poverty—that era ends with this book. After building a seven-figure business, coaching hundreds of entrepreneurs to do the same, and then answering a higher calling, Mel Pharr is possibly the only person on the planet who can lead this movement. Part permission slip, part profit plan, this book will do exactly what it promises - get you to six figures (or more!) talking to dead people!

—**Sara Connell,** Founder of Thought Leader Academy and bestselling author of *The Science of Getting Rich for Women*

When I found Mel, I instantly knew she was the mentor I'd been looking for. Her 5-Part Client Attraction Framework transformed my business. It's no surprise that she's combined her considerable talent as a business mentor with her rare gift as a medium. This book is a straightforward, literal blueprint for creating a thriving and profitable mediumship business that's sustainable and also feeds your soul. If that's what you're looking for, do everything she tells you to do in this book. I promise, it works!

—**Julie Kick,** Business Coach and Author of *Weathering the Grief Storm*

"I had no idea that being my authentic self could make me as rich as I've become. If I had, I would have done it a lot earlier."

—Oprah Winfrey

"It is not the creation of wealth that is wrong, but the love of money for its own sake."

—Margaret Thatcher

THE
PROFITABLE
SPIRITUAL
MEDIUM

HOW TO MAKE SIX FIGURES AND BEYOND TALKING TO DEAD PEOPLE

MELISSA PHARR

EVIDENTIAL SPIRITUAL MEDIUM

The Profitable Spiritual Medium: How to make six figures and beyond talking to dead people
© 2025 Melissa Pharr

Published by Thought Leader Academy Publishing
Thought Leader Academy Publishing
3901 N Kildare Ave
Chicago, Il 60641

Cover design by *the*BookDesigners
Interior design by Liz Schreiter

Hardback ISBN: 978-1-968668-11-2
Paperback ISBN: 978-1-968668-10-5
Ebook ISBN: 978-1-968668-12-9

*For my Mom. Thank you for showing
me what a woman who wastes no time
doubting herself can do. For my soulmate.
Rob, your unconditional love and unwavering
belief in me is the fuel that powers me.*

CONTENTS

INTRODUCTION

Seven months after I discovered my spiritual gifts as a medium, I began working professionally. My worst fear was becoming a self-proclaimed expert, and much too soon. After a conversation with a mentor of mine – who had been working as a professional medium for years – where she assured me it was time to charge for my work, I took the leap. I still remember her saying to me, "If you can give high-quality readings consistently six months in that another medium might take six years to be able to give, why wait?"

It's funny because that was the kind of conversation I'd been having with my own clients for nearly eight years during my time as an online marketing strategist. From 2014 through 2021 I ran my own business, coaching and consulting service-based female entrepreneurs to help them create six-figure, multi six-figure, and seven-figure businesses. By the end of that nearly eight-year stretch I'd sold 100s of courses online, created a marketing program for women from which more than 500 clients had graduated, and hosted live three-day events in New York City with attendees from all over the world, among other endeavors.

Something happens after you hear a client tell you that their target market is merely, wait for it… *people*," for the thousandth time. Suffice it to say that after eight years of begging my clients to be more specific and compelling with their marketing, I felt like I was having the same conversation on repeat. If there's one thing I know about myself, it's that once my own creativity and growth feels stifled, it's time to move on. That's why I shut down that business come 2021. I could sense a new chapter was approaching. My partner and I moved from New York City to Colorado and started a family. When our first daughter was born I'd taken two years off to focus on parenting and to discover what was next on my career path.

Becoming a medium was more of a shock to me than 40 hours of childbirth, if you can believe it. It came into my life with a bang and I said a solid yes to this path, putting my all into it.

It's true that my solid yes took a couple of months. Like many mediums who become aware of their ability to connect with spirits, I went through a series of what I thought were pretty wackadoodle happenings. It started with an out of body experience that felt like remembering being a medium in a past life. I remember the visitation from both of my passed grandmothers too, that was wild! Shortly after that, I unexpectedly connected with the spirit of a friends' father. As the events piled up, I hired two different mediums to see if, without telling them anything, they'd be able to validate what I'd experienced. They did, and that felt like a giant step forward in terms of making sure I wasn't going insane. Yup, wild things were beginning to happen. I felt strongly that I was getting constant signs from Spirit to strongly encourage me along this curious path.

My first full year in business, I was able to sell out every offer I made. Whether it was a private mediumship reading, a private spiritual assessment for an aspiring medium, a group training, or a 12-week development circle, every offer went. By the first quarter of my second year, I was creating $30,000 in revenue each quarter with a profit margin of nearly 70%, while working 28 hours a week and never on nights or weekends. Of those 28 hours, only 30% of them were spent working with clients—mediumship readings, spiritual assessments and development circles. Why is that significant? It's the reason I was able to write two books, create two courses, and birth a second human in 2025. I spent 70% of my time being creative and looking ahead to bring my next idea to life. I always make sure to avoid the dangerous entrepreneurial mistake of booking oneself solid with readings—trading dollars for hours—with no time to leverage a business, or even think about it, for that matter. Daymares of being booked every hour from 9am - 5pm with coaching clients in my past business had haunted me. It was enough for me to learn my lesson.

It wasn't long before my students were asking me if I would teach them how to make a living as a medium. Even with a small subscriber list of 500, an Instagram following of 450 people, and about 1,500 followers on YouTube, I began receiving email after email, from people I'd never met, asking me for business know-how for mediums.

Without trying to sound like an a-hole: it was pretty difficult to ignore how horribly most mediums I've known struggle with marketing. As the emails begging for help piled up, it was almost comical when I said out loud to myself, "I'm a marketer *and* I'm a medium. Well, shit Mel. How often does *that* happen?"

Not very often it turns out. I Googled "how to make money as a medium," and I can't say I was impressed with the turn out. In fact, this was near the top of my search.

820+ likes · 4 years ago

The Truth About Making Money on the Spiritual Path

Here's the blunt truth: You are not likely to make a lot of money on the spiritual path. Whether you're working as a healer, a psychic, a meditation instructor ...

Luckily, it's not true. On top of that, I realized how important it is to me to be helping people who are often empaths, humanitarians, and the healers of the world. Wouldn't it be nice if this brand of humans started being fairly compensated? When it really came down to it, I knew the strong pull to write this book and offer this help—that I'd been determined to ignore—truly felt like a call from

Spirit and not just something I was "shoulding" myself to do. Once I made the decision, it took about two seconds before the ideas and inspiration started pouring in. All of the most important things that I'd learned from teaching so many entrepreneurs to create businesses they truly loved came to mind. Not only could I run my own business in a way that was far more enjoyable and efficient than my last, but I could teach other mediums to do it too.

 If you're just starting out developing your skills as a medium, I strongly recommend that you check out my first book, *Speaking With Spirits* by using the QR code. *Speaking With Spirits* generously shares my straightforward system for bringing your mediumistic skills to wow level.

Going pro prematurely isn't sexy. More importantly, it can do a lot of damage if you prioritize making money over creating a high-quality and potentially life-changing experience for your sitter.

In contrast, *this* book is for you if you're ready to become a professional medium and you want a step-by-step approach from someone who's done it. I'll be sharing absolutely every detail of my journey and I hold nothing back. I'm an everyone-wins-when-we-all-do-better type of girl.

If you're someone who asks yourself, "Who would want to work with li'l ol' me when there are plenty of other amazing mediums out there?", you can expect to discover fun ways to differentiate yourself from other mediums and spiritual practitioners. I'll be walking you through exactly what to take action on to make sure you're focused on client-getting tasks so you can escape bright shiny object syndrome that keeps you feeling like a squirrel... who's broke.

Yes, I will break everything down, step-by-step, because that's how I do. Things like creating content or naming your offer that has boggled your mind in the past will feel easier and come more quickly once you've read this book. From creating and pricing your offers, to hearing yes from the kind of people you love working with, you'll learn everything you need to know to attract a following, create amazing client and collaborator relationships, and make a living without working a stupid amount of hours each week.

Guess what else? No cold calls or anything sleezy. It's very possible that you won't even need to have sales calls with potential clients. But, if you do, I've got that part covered too.

Best of all, you can be a medium who makes a living and still be yourself. There are just five categories to focus on each week to be creating revenue in your business and you can do them in a way that works for you. If you want to supercharge this read by getting your hands on this free training, *Top 3 Mistakes Mediums Make When It Comes To Making Money*, that isn't even available on my YouTube channel, you can use the QR code.

Before we continue, it's essential that I share with you the definitions of a few terms that I'll be using throughout this book. In my time talking to dead people and through my studies with mentors that I respect and trust, I've come to believe that we are all connected as one through consciousness. This all one consciousness that continues after the death of the physical body is what I call the Spirit World and will reference throughout this book as Spirit with a capital S. Think of this all one consciousness as the mothership of all of our individual spirits that come together as one.

When I am speaking about an individual spirit, or a group of individual spirits that are communicating with me as a medium, I will use the word spirit, or spirits, with a lower case s. It's important to note that different people have different belief systems and for some, they speak or pray to Spirit, while others may reference this same all one consciousness as God, Source, or another term. Others believe in both God and Spirit, but view them separately.

Lastly, if I speak about "transitioning" or "passing" this means dying. If I mention the "other side," I'm talking about where we go after we die to join the mothership of all one consciousness, the Spirit World. When I use the term "sitter," I'm not talking about childcare. I'm referring to the person who *sits* with a medium to receive a reading. Finally, a "spiritual impression" is a single thought that a spirit sends to a medium via any of the clair senses in order to communicate.

Without further ado, let's start transforming you into a profitable spiritual medium.

PART I

HAVING THE COURAGE TO MAKE A LIVING AS A MEDIUM

When students come to my courses or development circle for the first time and I ask the question, "Who here has ever felt like you're about to shit your pants before you give a reading?" I always see the slow-motion hand raise from the majority of students while they check their surroundings in our Zoom room to make sure they're not the only one. After that, smiles break out on the faces of my students, chuckles or full on truck-stop laughter explode the silence, and mutual respect and camaraderie becomes the culture of our group.

I don't do this *just* to be funny. Mediumship is a vulnerable thing and the stakes usually feel pretty high. We are, afterall, talking about death, right? The truth of the matter is that there are about 101 reasons that people who get the call from Spirit say no for a while, or sometimes for forever.

They are afraid of what other people will think. Depending on where they live in the world and who their friends and family are, mediumship could pave the way to a path of utter isolation. I've seen it and it sucks.

They're worried it's time to become institutionalized. This was me when I first became aware of my mediumistic skills. I legit worried that my intermittent anxiety had progressed to a *more* serious mental health disorder that I'd need additional support for.

They find other mediums or mediumship classes to be unsafe spaces or too competitive in terms of skill level, so I've heard. And this from mediums, right? The "spiritual" ones who are meant to be prioritizing the healing of their sitters. It's just plain silly if you ask me.

When it comes to working professionally as a medium, well, just forget it! That would mean accepting payment for something that a significant percentage of the population thinks is straight up cuckoo!

Along with these roadblocks are plenty of other common mistakes that mediums make when it comes to the journey to go pro. While so many are profoundly skilled at speaking to Spirit, just as many of us struggle with the know-how to actually create a decent living out of our work.

Choosing the mediumship path can demand ovaries and balls of steel in many cases. Good news. By the end of this book, I think you'll be able to reach into your pants and find that things have become pretty sturdy down there.

CHAPTER 1

FROM ONLINE MARKETER TO SPIRITUAL MEDIUM

It all started on October 22nd in 2022. My relationship with Spirit was a fast-paced one that finally culminated almost two months later with what I call my "holy shit" reading. If you've read my book *When Spirits Speak*, you know what happened when I sat down with a near stranger to see if I was crazy, or if it was true that mediums were real, and I might be one.

Her name was Abby and she was hosting a local mama meetup. I'd seen her a few times and felt a connection. She is a practicing doula and the sort of person who is so very present and kind, a natural caregiver. I felt compelled to tell her what I'd been going through and got the inkling from Spirit that she would be the perfect person to help me test out any mediumistic abilities I might have.

A week later we sat in my family room. I made sure to be honest and transparent about my absolute lack of experience, but my dire need to see what might happen. She was clear on the situation and fully ready. I wanted to manage her expectations so I told her to be prepared for ten minutes of absolute silence and nothing but a whole lot of diddly dick happening.

I began by quieting my mind as I would if I were sitting in meditation. At first there was nothing, just silence and the odd sound of a settling house. Then, within moments, I noticed the feeling of fuzzy energy on my right side. The thing that I'll never forget was how it blew my mind just *how subtle* the tiny inklings of communication from a spirit actually are. So subtle indeed that if you've never been told, you'd easily miss it altogether or feel certain that it was merely your imagination. The first thing I understood about the energy that I was sensing was that it was feminine. This spirit had been a woman when she was living. As I leaned into these sensations, the fuzzy energy split in two and although I wasn't quite sure, I decided to trust my interpretation that was leading me to believe there were two spirits present. Within moments, I sensed and *knew* that her grandmother and aunt, both on her mother's side, were present. I can't say how I knew, except that in my mind's eye I caught quick glimpses of their stature and some facial features, however obscurely they were coming across. I also got the feel of an aunt-like figure and a grandmother-like figure, the same way that you would if you met someone and they came across in that way.

The moment I relayed their identity, Abby burst into tears and began nodding her head. Somewhere in the mix I got up to grab a box of tissues that luckily was nearby. As I shared what was coming to me, more information from these spirits followed. I knew details of their passing and the timing, their character and personality, and their closest living family members.

At one point when I felt connected to her grandmother, I saw a short video reel up and off to my right side in my mind. It was her grandmother's thumbs and pointer fingers holding a necklace that she was swinging back and forth. On the necklace was something round. I was in awe as I identified this round item as a small silver medal from a vocal competition I'd won in high school. I knew in that moment somehow that that object, of course, wasn't what was hanging from her grandmother's necklace, but that she was communicating to me that the object being round was significant. When I told Abby this she gasped loudly as her hand went to her mouth.

"I have that necklace at my house right now. My grandmother's wedding ring is hanging from it!" I was in too much shock to remember a lot of details about my reaction to the necklace, but I'm pretty sure I was only a few seconds away from shitting myself. Even so, it just kept coming. I saw a knitted shawl of some kind next and described it to Abby. She told me it was hanging over a chair at her house and that she hadn't washed it because it smelled like her grandmother. I was shown memories of the end of life goodbye for her aunt who was laid in a hospital bed, unresponsive, with family members sharing their farewells. I told Abby that her aunt had heard and understood those words and tears continued to pour down her face.

As the reading went on, the information flowed and I lost track of time, but I do recall how it ended. When the information slowed and the most important messages felt as if they had been delivered, I told Abby that I was ready to leave her with their love. We paused for a moment in utter silence. I remember one of us saying, "Holy shit!" and within an instant we both burst into hardcore ugly cries that were cathartic and filled with love, healing, and excitement. For Abby, perhaps it was something she had already believed in and had an understanding of, but for me, I was in awe of the apparent way that this world worked and the magic that surrounds us that I'd known almost nothing about.

I was in disbelief. How could I feel *who* they were and *how* they were so easily? Not only that, but I was able to relay messages from both of these spirits that were incredibly meaningful and significant not just to Abby, but to her mother, who texted me shortly after the reading to give her thanks. Abby sent a text as well, with pictures of the shawl and necklace that I had seen.

Photos courtesy of Melissa Pharr

When Rob came down the steps from his office after Abby left, he must have seen the dazed and shocked look on my face as I struggled to process what had just happened.

"Are you ok?" he inquired. I was silent for a beat and then, "You're not gonna fuckin' believe what just happened." I breathed as I shook my head incredulously.

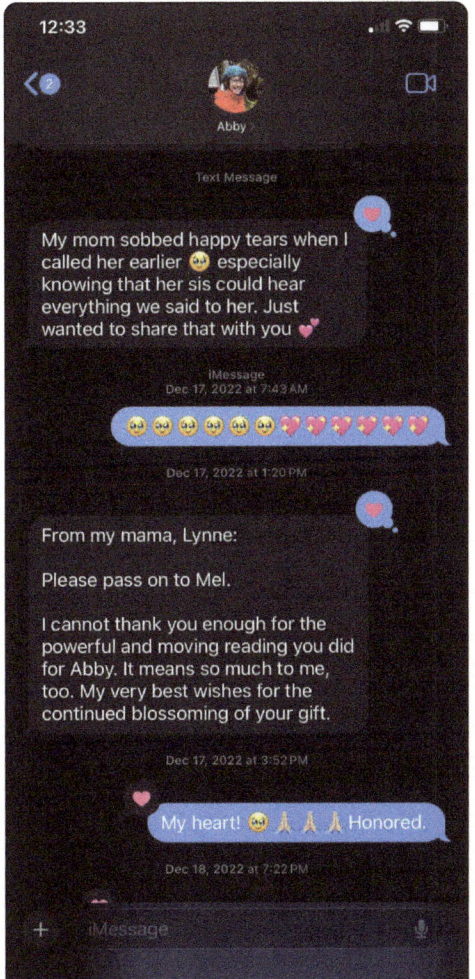

Photos courtesy of Melissa Pharr

• • •

It's funny how sometimes every step of your life seems to have led and prepared you for what comes next. When I retired from my previous business as an online marketing strategist and spent two years being a stay at home mom, I was anxious to discover what was next for me. I fantasized about what I'd do differently if I were to start another business from the beginning. By the time those two years passed, I knew *exactly* what I'd do differently and how I'd be far more efficient in terms of creating revenue faster, and with a more significant profit margin. It turns out that my plan was a good one. Not only does my current business as a medium allow me to love my work, spend ample time with my family, and take care of my body, mind, and soul—my top priorities—it's allowed me to create six figures and beyond.

But don't be fooled into thinking that I popped out of my mother this way. There were years of blood, sweat, and tears that taught me how to do better this go around. Let me bring you back with me to the winter of 2015, a.k.a my season of emotional and financial disaster. After a roller coaster of an entrepreneurial journey that had begun in 2009 and gone through several different iterations, this was the grand finale storm before the calm that is now my life.

I was in a hotel in Sydney, Australia for a conference. I was most definitely supposed to be happy. All of my fellow entrepreneurs were heading up to the rooftop bar of the hotel where you could see an eye candy view of the Sydney Opera House. They'd be mingling and laughing. They'd be dressed sexy-business-casual. Meanwhile, I was *this* close to having an anxious nervous breakdown. I logged into my bank account. There was less than $100 in my checking account. I never used my checking account at this point except to pay off miniscule amounts from my credit card bills. Yes, bills. After years of counting every penny that I put into my entrepreneurial endeavors and rarely hiring mentors or team members to help me, I'd decided to shit or get off the pot. I'd opened three different zero interest credit cards in addition to my primary business credit card and personal credit card to sign up for two tiers of a high-level coaching program with a business mentor. Luckily, before I'd become the current financial disaster that I was, I'd had good enough credit to qualify. So far a whole lot of diddly dick was going right. I totaled up the debt that I'd racked up over the previous months from my personal expenses and business investments. It totaled more than $42,000.

What's worse is that I'd finished three sales calls in a row that afternoon from the hotel room and none of them had said yes. Two of them had said flat out nos, and the final call ended with my potential client saying they'd get back to me. I had little faith though. I'd heard that line many times at this point and no one ever did get back to me.

My entrepreneurial friend and roommate could tell something was off with me. I certainly wasn't my joking, playful, bubbly usual self.

"Are you ready to go?" She asked inquisitively, but cautious. I was in my dress with my hair and makeup done.

"I don't think I'm going to go." I managed to choke out just before a tear drop rolled down each of my cheeks.

"What's wrong Mel?" She looked sympathetic and her empathy cracked the wall that was holding all of my overwhelming emotions and anxiety inside. I burst into anxious sobs, drawing shallow and stuttering clunky breaths in between.

"I can't spend any money and I don't want to drink or be around anyone. I'm in so much debt. I just don't know if this is *ever* going to work for me!"

It's difficult for me to remember much more. I'm pretty sure I blocked out a lot of the details from that time in my life and definitely any specifics from the rest of that conversation. She did her best to reassure me, but my downward spiral was momentous and there was no turning it around. She said a quiet goodbye as she went to join everyone else and I collapsed on my bed for a good ugly cry session that I'm sure lasted 20 minutes or more. If you've ever ugly cried that hard you know it's exhausting. It's the kind that involves your whole body—more rigorous than violent hiccups that won't stop. My flight, my share of the hotel room, the food during the trip—it was all going on the credit card with the most wiggle room and I had no idea if and when I'd be able to pay it off.

. . .

Three days later, the conference was over. It had been a 72-hour roller coaster experience. I was becoming more inspired every day by the conversations I was having with my entrepreneur friends and the success stories that many of them shared. Then I'd check my email, hoping for a new client, and avoid looking at my bank account, which often led to more tears. While there was a lot of up and down, I was in a better place overall, having put together a new plan with the ideas I'd garnered from other women's stories and the training and exercises that we'd practiced. I had a new plan that I intended to bring home with me and a fraction of hope as well. Even though I couldn't afford it, my friends and I had decided to rent an Airbnb in Sydney for a few days after the conference. We'd traveled so far it seemed to make sense even if financially it wasn't the best choice. We sat around the kitchen table at the house checking our email before we planned to venture out to the beach for a walk. My inbox was empty. I carried my laptop into my bedroom to put my things away when all of a sudden a new email popped into my inbox. It read: "Cha-Ching! Somebody bought something."

I'll never forget that moment of surprise and pure joy that electrified my entire body. The only time *that* email would show up in my inbox was when someone registered for my private coaching program. I held my breath as I opened the email. The final sales call I'd had before my breakdown in the hotel room had finally paid off. The woman who said she'd get back to me *did*, and she'd decided to work with me! I've just about always been described as a passionate and enthusiastic person, and the full on scream of elation that came out of me made all of my friends jump and turn to me with wide eyes.

"She signed up! The woman I spoke with who said she'd get back to me signed up!" My voice was piercing and shrill. I couldn't contain my excitement and the thrilling feeling of alignment that resonated throughout my entire body. We all cheered and I did an obnoxious full on song and dance around the living room complete with pelvic thrusts, booty shakes, and I'm sure, some tits out moments. While I was far from paying off my massive credit card debt, something changed in that moment when this small step forward demonstrated to me that *something* I'd done over the past five agonizing months had worked. After all, I hadn't failed at having people reach out to me for a sales conversation about working together. Even if my conversion rate wasn't sky high at the moment, I was getting people to knock on the door.

As we enjoyed our final days down under, I found myself relaxing and having an ounce of faith restored within me. It wasn't more than a week later that I began a steady practice of meditation to start each work day. I had to get my head on straight and calm my nerves to keep the little momentum that I'd gained going. I suppose it didn't seem like anything special at the time, but by the end of every short five-minute meditation session, I had a clear and simple list of actions to take that day. They were simple things, like:

- Following up with every potential client I'd had a sales call with but hadn't heard from
- Creating a juicy online post and sharing my opt-in at the end to build my following bit by bit
- Making a short one to two-minute video story with a great sales tip that I'd just used successfully

- Coming up with a free mini-coaching call titled "Master Your Money Conversations 20-Minute Assessment" about how to invite ideal clients to say yes to working with you

I could get most of these types of daily tasks done in two to three hours and I started to see my calendar filled with "discovery calls"—what I called sales conversations with prospective clients. Instead of feeling like I was frenzied and frazzled doing every little thing possible to get clients each and every day, all day long, I started to hone in on the whispered list of inspired actions that would download into my mind after each meditation session.

I sat down at my desk one morning and it came to me clearly and quickly. I had unknowingly created a framework that was guiding my daily actions in my business. It was a Client Attraction Framework. When I reflected and really broke it down, I realized that I'd been taking actions each day that fell into one of five client-attracting categories. At this point I had a steady stream of prospects coming my way, so I knew it was working. Additionally, as I had more and more discovery call conversations, I began to realize how to show my excitement for each potential client and transparently walk them through my process that I knew could help them avoid some of the dead ends I'd met. My passion and enthusiasm began to take the place of the desperation and survival mentality that I'd been drowning in, and likely projecting, before my mini breakthrough when that first client signed on in February of 2015.

Over the following spring months, I continued my plan and worked my 5-Part Client Attraction Framework, which I'll be sharing with you in detail in Part II of this book! I made a few thousand dollars in March, more in April, and a whopping $0 in May. I panicked a little during that $0 May, but over the summer, my sales increased each month. I remember August being a $69,000 revenue month by selling nine private coaching packages at $6,000 each and two more at $7,500 each. In September of 2015, I opened up the first run of my live business program *Underearner to Unforgettable,* or U2U as I came to call it, and created over $100K in revenue. By the end of 2015 I'd earned more than $250,000 in revenue and paid off all three zero interest credit cards as well as my original business credit card and my personal credit card. It was by far the biggest turning point I'd experienced. It felt like a long time coming after years of on and off financial struggle that had accompanied my previous entrepreneurial endeavors since 2009.

When I think about all of the invaluable lessons I've learned over the course of my entrepreneurial journey, I feel overwhelmingly grateful for the struggles that taught me to innovate and find creative solutions. The confidence that grew within me is something that has made my journey into mediumship much easier than you might think. I've had to rely on myself for so many years now that the level of trust I have in myself, and in something greater—whether you call it Spirit, God, Source, etc.—is pretty darn solid. And conveniently, I've discovered that trusting yourself, and trusting Spirit, is one of the keys to mediumship. Maybe that's part of why I've been what you might call a "quick study" as a medium.

Unfortunately, another thing I've discovered upon entering the world of mediumship, is that most mediums find it difficult, if not excruciatingly painful, to confidently charge for their services. Even if they are able to be fairly paid for their work, many of them have confided in me that being business-minded isn't their strongest suit. Usually they are trading dollars for hours and those hours of work aren't sustainable long-term because speaking with spirits requires energy—lots of it! It's not the kind of job you can work from 9am - 5pm, Monday through Friday.

As much as I thought I'd never be teaching business and marketing strategy again, it couldn't be more obvious to me that I'm being called to use these skills to help guide and support spiritual practitioners. The purpose that powers my mediumship is to be a part of ending division in my country and in our world. In this world that we live in, whether you like it or not, money is a powerful tool. If you ask me, I'd love to see more of it in the hands of the people I know who have the most empathy, compassion, and desire to help heal others through our heartfelt and life-changing service that we offer as mediums.

CHAPTER 2

WHY MEDIUMSHIP AND MONEY MIX

always knew I'd write at least one book and for years, I thought it would be about women and money. In fact, the motivation behind my work as an online marketing strategist was to help more people, primarily women, overcome financial inequities and attain financial freedom. From my entrepreneurial perspective, I planned on sharing my knowledge to help women overcome money shame, become confident earners, and conduct high-integrity sales conversations without the sleaze. My passion for this work became even stronger when I discovered that more than 50% of my clients were mothers, and due to taking on the majority of childrearing responsibilities, they could rarely take advantage of the same career and personal growth opportunities as their partner.

The thing about money is that when we hear the word, we often associate it with greed and the proclivity to be ostentatious with one's wealth. Perhaps you feel that you have a healthy relationship with money and that you don't automatically attach negative connotations to it. Still, it's undeniable that an undercurrent of negative belief systems regarding money are a part of the fabric of most modern day societies.

Yep, money gets a bad rap doesn't it? It's no wonder. We often see it used in ways that do display greed and power-mongering. But hasn't money shame become a bit archaic by now? And if it's not archaic for you, I'll be as bold as to say that it *should* be.

Why? Because when it comes down to it, money is just a tool. You can use it for good, or you can use it for evil, and anything in between. Has having money led some people to be greedy and power hungry? Absolutely, but I'll tell you that I've met rich people who are assholes and poor people who are assholes—rich people who are wonderful humans and poor people who are far more kind and generous than the wealthiest people on this planet. What I do know is that money continues to be something we need to survive, and I feel strongly compelled to help humanitarians have a hell of a lot more of it. To put it plainly, don't waste your time blaming the dollars. Instead, go ahead and blame the douche canoes who use money to yield every kind of injustice. Then, decide *not* to be one yourself, and make some money of your own.

The next layer of this conversation is dealing with the idea that perhaps mediumship is too spiritual to mix with money. This undoubtedly ties into the idea that because money cannot be a sacred or spiritual thing, that mediumship might become tainted when charged for. But why can't money be a sacred or spiritual thing? It's one of the most important tools for survival that exists. It can do a whole lot of good and create massive change for the better, depending on whose hands it's in. Perhaps your brain agrees, but you struggle because you know that there are many who don't have much money. Should the healing gift of mediumship be inaccessible to them? No. I'll speak to this more in Part I of this book, but for now, I'll say that there are many ways for any person to receive a high quality mediumship reading without having to pay.

The big question that many of us ask is, 'Does charging for your services diminish the spiritual nature of this work?' Absolutely not.

Does being fraudulent in this work destroy the spiritual aspect? Of course. Keep in mind that being paid for your services and being fraudulent are two very different things. That's true in absolutely every industry and with every service. Too many people confuse the two! Think of the energy that you use as a medium, why shouldn't you be compensated for your work, especially given how life-changing it can be for others, and for the better.

Even for mediums who *are* charging for their services, the majority of them don't get rich doing this work, and many don't even earn a living that is significant enough for them to live comfortably given the current cost of living. In 2025, ZipRecruiter reported that the average salary for a psychic medium is $66,464 per year, with most earning between $37,500 (25th percentile) and $97,500 (90th percentile).

The beautiful thing about helping more mediums see that they too can make a difference and a living with their work, is that it still aligns with that passionate purpose of mine to help more women have financial equality *and* to get money into the hands of people who care about people. All research and industry data that is available points to the majority of spiritual mediums being women. That's no surprise to me. In my first year teaching mediumship with 42 mediums registering for my development circles each quarter, I rarely had more than one man per class of 14.

If it puzzles you why this is such an important task for me, consider that in 2023 -2024, according to *The Institute for Women's Policy Research*, women working full-time, year-round in the U.S. earned about 82.7 to 83.6 cents for every dollar earned by men, reflecting a gender pay gap of roughly 16–17%. Sadly, this gap has widened slightly from 2022, when women earned 84 cents on the dollar, marking the first significant setback in two decades. Over a 40-year career, the average American woman could lose hundreds of thousands to over a million dollars in earnings due to the pay gap.

These gaps are likely even wider given the wage disparity between white women and women of color.

What's wild is that even with women getting a smaller part of the overall cookie, they are still playing a larger role in philanthropy than men. According to a research and insights report out of Fidelity Charitable, women are more likely than men to give to charity and to volunteer their time, with 91% of high-net-worth women reporting charitable giving compared to 87% of high-net-worth men.

But if you have a penis, breasts, or both, have no fear. All genders, and humans for that matter, matter to me. All those who are here to make the world a better place with their dollars, time, energy, and beyond, are humans I'm happy to support. Ultimately, it's been left up to us to find a way to live a financially sustainable life via our spiritual profession and the purpose of this book is to help you do just that.

CHAPTER 3

THE TOP THREE MISTAKES MEDIUMS MAKE

While I consider myself an optimist and often like to focus on the positive aspects of achieving my goals, I've found after many years of being an online marketing strategist that being aware of the most prominent pitfalls goes an awfully long way. You have to know what to look out for when you begin building your mediumship business. Efficiency is important in the practice of mediumship, and it's just as important when you decide to turn your craft into something that will allow you to make a comfortable living. As entrepreneurs, many of us don't have unlimited resources of time, money, or energy. When we finally do feel courageous enough to take the leap and start receiving payment for our services, there's a limited runway for takeoff. You've got to use your resources wisely to ensure that you don't run out of fuel and crash and burn. I've known countless entrepreneurs who have spent hours, days, weeks, and months ripping their hair out while designing their website. Sadly, they've failed at using their time to connect with potential clients or take client-getting actions and the website isn't what they wanted or compelling to their ideal client. Now, they're out of money, time, and motivation.

Sound familiar? Or maybe you—I mean *they*—had the brilliant idea to launch a course and spent months designing the content only to have no one sign up? There's a reasonable explanation for why things like this happen and we'll dive into that explanation shortly when I tell you what to do instead of making the three most common mistakes. In this book, you'll hear me say repeatedly that you *must* spend time on client-attracting activities. The good news is that by the time you finish this read, you'll know exactly what qualifies as a client-attracting activity, and what doesn't.

Perhaps you've had the experience of being told what *not* to do, or even *what* to do, but you feel that the *how* of it all is never clear enough. Maybe the *how* has ultimately always been the part that leaves you stuck, overwhelmed, and frustrated. I get it. I've been there many times. That's why I want to let you know right from the start that I plan to cover everything I wish I'd known when I first began my entrepreneurial journey. I know it would have saved me from quite a few shit show experiences as a business owner. In fact, my promise to you is that not only will I tell you about these mistakes and what to do *instead,* in part two of this book we'll get into the *how* of building your mediumship business.

Let's talk about the top three mistakes I see many mediums making that makes or breaks their ability to not only make enough money to survive, but to enjoy their work in a way that feels fulfilling and sustainable in an energetic, emotional, and creative way.

MISTAKE #1: TRYING TO PROFIT AND SCALE BY TRADING MORE DOLLARS FOR HOURS

I had a medium in my development circle for a couple of rounds and it was an absolute honor to work with her. She was such an incredible medium: she could quickly identify the spirit, receive evidence consistently and accurately, and showcased wonderful presentation skills. I can't remember how she ended up with a bonus medium-ship coaching session from me, but as we began, she announced that she was hoping it was okay to talk about the business aspect of mediumship.

It turns out she worked a corporate job and did mediumship on the side. Her dream was to leave her corporate job and work full-time as a medium. In addition to having a full-time job and working part-time as a medium, she was also a parent, so you can imagine that she had limited time on her hands. She was incredibly intelligent but when it came to scaling her business and making enough money to quit her job, she was struggling to get there.

Although she had a small audience, she had no trouble finding clients who wanted to pay her for her readings. The problem was that she was giving so many readings that she was spending 100% of her precious time working as a medium trading dollars for hours. Not only did she lack any offers that allowed her to leverage her time and revenue, but she lacked time and space to think, plan, strategize, and create and market offers that served more than one client at time.

I pointed this out and crunched some numbers to show her that there was little hope, if any, of replacing her salary and leaving her corporate job by giving *more* private readings. Most importantly, she would be exhausted on just about every level if she pushed her-self to the max by giving more readings.

While different mediums have different energetic capacity for readings, I don't know *any* who are making a living by trading dollars for hours by only offering private one-on-one readings. The only exception might be famous mediums who read for celebrities and charge a pretty penny that is beyond what most mediums get paid. Even if you do fall into this category, you're likely an outlier, and I'll wager that it's not the most fulfilling way to be a professional medium. I've heard story after story of mediums who gave massive amounts of readings and after a year, they were burnt out and needed a break. Most of them ran into mental health issues or expressed physical symptoms and usually they experienced both!

Remember that mediumship is about working with energy, *lots* of it! That means that it requires a lot from us and for most people, isn't suited to be treated as a nine to five. The mediums I know who have tried to work in this way tend to be reading past their energetic threshold, hit burnout, and feel unfulfilled by their work. On top of that, recall that the average yearly salary of a medium is $66,464 per year!

I don't know about you, but burnt out and broke is not where I want to be or how I want to feel. I never want to lose the magic and awe of being a medium. I made a promise to myself early on that I'd only give as many private readings each week as would allow me to love my work and look forward to each time I sit down with someone to bring their passed loved ones through. In my mind, enjoying your work and creating your business in a way that will be sustainable for the long term is an absolute must.

To give you a concrete example of how giving one-on-one readings often falls short in terms of creating a profitable business and being sustainable on many levels, imagine that you charge $500 a reading. Then imagine that you give five readings a week, four weeks a month. As an aside, I give three readings a week. Could I give more? Sure. Do I want to? No. I like to enjoy every reading and balance that work with things like writing books, teaching development circles and courses, public speaking, etc. Not to mention that these other things I spend my time on allow me to leverage my business in a big way.

With our example of five readings a week at $500, over the course of a year you'd create $110,000 in revenue. That may not sound too bad, but remember that that's revenue, not profit. You'd still need to subtract all of your business expenses, pay taxes, and finally see what's left over for personal spending. Even if you were charging $350 a reading, at five readings a week, four weeks a month, you'd earn $84,000 in revenue. For most of us living in this world that's not going to cut it, especially if you have a family to feed.

In addition, let's consider the other things that would need to be in place to make it feasible to give 20, $500 readings a month.

You'd need the confidence to charge that price. While these mediums exist, the average rate for a reading is not $500. Most often I see $350 as the high end of what mediums might charge for a reading with most of them charging between $100 - $300. I've taught hundreds of mediums, and I can tell you that charging for a reading adds pressure which means you have to have a high level of confidence. Building confidence like that is a significant part of the journey.

You'd need an audience with the willingness to invest at that price. Most mediums I know aren't great at marketing so the vast majority of them haven't spent a significant amount of time growing a following. To book five sessions a week, every week, for a year at the $500 price point would require a sizable audience. Even if you have put time into growing a subscriber base, and you get lots of referrals, acquiring high quality leads isn't an overnight thing and takes time.

You'd have to be sold out at that price all the time. This really goes hand in hand with needing an audience. Five readings a week, four weeks a month comes out to 240 readings per year. A lot of the mediums I know don't even have a subscriber list of 240 people, nevermind that only a percentage of your followers are likely to buy. Online marketing statistics show that usually only 2% - 5% of subscribers or social media followers become purchasers when encountering an offer that costs ~$300 and often the percentage is even less. Even with mediumship being a great referral-based business, being sold out at that rate continuously would require a significant audience.

You'd have to be consistently at the top of your game. Remember that mediumship requires a lot of energy and that life happens. There will always be times that you need to cancel, don't feel well, or might go through tough experiences that make it nearly impossible to give a reading. I've known mediums who have had to take a break for various reasons, including grieving the loss of their own passed loved one or just going through a hard time emotion-

ally, mentally, physically, etc. I have a YouTube video titled, *I Lost My Gifts (My Dark Night Of The Soul),* that shares transparently about a time that my anxiety got the better of me and forced me to take a break from mediumship. You can watch the video here using the QR code.

MISTAKE #2: GETTING SUCKED INTO THE LOW-WEALTH CONSCIOUSNESS OF THE MEDIUMSHIP INDUSTRY

Before I even get to the "crunching your numbers" part of the conversation, we have to face an additional barrier that many mediums struggle with. That struggle is undercharging—often due to undervaluing their services, among other things—and sometimes suffering from a feeling of guilt or fear for even *thinking* about charging for their work. Have you felt either of these things? Or both? If so, you're not alone. If not, you're rare! After coaching hundreds of entrepreneurs, I can tell you that I'm up against this more often than not.

Here's the truth, we have been royally fucked emotionaly and mentally when it comes to being able to have a clean and objective approach to our relationship with money. So much so that a significant amount of this book is dedicated to helping you understand why it's this way, and more importantly, why it doesn't *need* to be this way. If you want to be able to enjoy making a living as a medium, you're going to have to have a deeper understanding about your relationship with money and work through all your feels so that you can open yourself up to receive payment for the incredible work that you do.

So let's start here. If you want to know why money might be a tricky topic for you, and why it *is* a tricky topic for so many people, consider this: A lot of us think about money in a negative way at times, as if it's a representation of greed or selfishness for those who have a lot of it. Conversely, we may also have experienced seeing some people who make a lot of money as impressive, powerful, and smart. If you have a lot of money, maybe you feel proud of the abundance you have if you feel you've earned it, or guilty if it was given to you. For those who don't have much at all, they might feel embarrassment or shame or even be treated as if they are lazy, and less valuable than those who have resources. And yet there are times that people make the assumption that if you don't have much, you must be a good and pious person who has their priorities straight. Whether or not you view money through any of these emotional lenses, I can promise you that they exist and are far more common, and often unconscious, than you might think. With this in mind, it's no wonder that when it comes to charging for your services, there can be a lot of big feelings that come up, like shame, excitement, fear, anxiety, pride, joy, or anger. I strongly encourage you to think of memories where you've felt any of the feelings I've described above and get curious about why that is. What does that say about your own relationship with money? How might you have to change the way you view money to make yourself more willing to accept it when you do good work?

While I could write a book on this topic alone, let's focus on the most common reasons that some people struggle with low-wealth consciousness and might feel nervous and afraid to charge for their work as a medium.

It's sensitive work with high stakes. We're talking to dead people here so yes, the stakes can feel pretty high and being a medium can come with significant pressure at times. You might have a sitter in front of you who is still heavily grieving their passed loved one. There could be sensitive information that comes through from a spirit. Something private might reveal itself in a reading. While these things are all true, does it mean that a medium shouldn't be paid? Aren't there other careers that are high stakes and sensitive? Consider a surgeon, EMT, ambulance driver, or firefighter. All of these professionals expect to be paid and there seems to be far less guilt or fear about receiving money for their work. While EMTs, ambulance drivers and firefighters are arguably underpaid, surgeons are among the highest paid medical professionals—and phew, talk about high stakes and sensitive work!

Keep in mind that high-quality mediumship holds the potential for the receiver to have a positive, life-changing experience. Due to how valuable this work is and how much energy it takes, shouldn't we be focused on earning what feels like an equal exchange instead of feeling shameful and resistant to receiving something that we all need to survive in this world? Remember that $37,500 is the yearly pay of a medium in the 25th percentile of average medium earnings. Did you know that that is only $5,350 over the 2025 federal poverty guidelines?

Mediumship is too sacred or spiritual to be a paid service. There are many spiritual or sacred practices and services that are paid. Some of those that I consider sacred are priests, wedding or funeral officiants, therapists, and teachers. These are all people who are doing meaningful work and some of it requires quite a bit of heavy emotional lifting or holding a sacred space for people to grieve, heal, and grow. The thing that I find disappointing is that all of these professions are paid very little for the positive impact that they have on individuals and society at large. It makes you wonder why we've learned to value these things financially in such a small way. Is there something about a service being sacred or spiritual that means it shouldn't mix with money? Does money make it less spiritual or sacred?

It turns out there's a reason. The priesthood aside, many of these fields I've just named are traditionally female-dominated, and we know that women are generally paid less than men for the same job. This fact is just one reason why many have come to believe that money makes mediumship less spiritual.

Remember that money is just a tool, and something that all of us need to survive in this world. If we value the spiritual and sacred aspect of our lives and value money in this world as one of the most important and vital tools that exists, then why don't we compensate the people who do this valuable work in a way that matches their contribution? Now that you know more about why this happens, isn't it high time that those who possess empathy, compassion, patience, and kindness, get paid? Wouldn't it be nice if they were well compensated for spreading the good they do for others?

If I'm not 100% accurate 100% of the time should I be paid? Yes, you should. However, my guidelines for when it's time to get paid are that 90% of the readings you give should be full of evidence that has an accuracy rate of 90% or higher. I didn't read that somewhere or have a mentor tell me, I just know that that's what I would expect if I were to get a paid reading. It's important to also accept that not all readings will go the way you want them to. I promise you that your career as a medium will always include what I call "shit show readings." This might be because the sitter is tricky to read for and your confidence plummets or that you have a hard time sensing a spirit and you're not sure why.

I remember the time I got on Zoom to give a reading and two people showed up. They both must have had PhDs in how to maintain deadpan expressions at all costs. My first mistake was asking if they were siblings.

"We're husband and wife!" The man declared roughly. Whoops! I guess my psychic skills failed me on that one, but I promise you I didn't sense any romantic vibes between the two of them and I just *might* have been bull's-eye-right about that one. I also told him I would say a spiritual intention-sort-of-prayer out loud before the reading if that was ok with them. The man asked me if it was a Christian prayer. When I told him "not really" he said, "You best keep that to yourself then."

Things were going downhill fast and I got nos to just about everything I shared with them. The only exception was when his mother in spirit said that he was about as stubborn as they get and his wife finally cracked a huge toothy smile and said, "Well *that* one's definitely true!"

Any medium who tells you that this never happens to them is full of shit. Period. That being said, as you practice and reach higher levels of proficiency, these things happen less and less often and you learn how to navigate a slew of different situations with your sitters and with Spirit.

In fact, if we decided to *only* pay any sort of professional for being 100% accurate 100% of the time, a lot of people wouldn't be paid for their work! Consider economists or meteorologists who study the atmosphere and weather patterns to forecast the weather. While meteorologists are quite accurate for short-term forecasts (90%+ for 3-5 days), their accuracy drops significantly for forecasts beyond 10 days, where they're correct only about *half* the time. Unlike meteorologists, economists' 23% accuracy rate is dramatically lower!

What about doctors? Haven't you heard stories from friends or even had experiences where a visit to the doctor resulted in poor advice or a diagnosis which was dead wrong? No pun intended. Project managers have jobs that are a lot like herding cats. Can you imagine how often things might go awry when you're managing multiple people?

These comparisons aren't made to encourage you to lower your expectations regarding the quality of your work. They're made to support you in being realistic instead of becoming a perfectionist and holding yourself back from being compensated as any other professional does, and should, for work that's well done.

I share this to highlight people's unrealistic expectations of psychics and mediums. There is a misconception that when a medium walks down the street, they see dead people surrounding the person walking by them, without even focusing their mind on Spirit. That's not how it works. Due to a lack of understanding that many mediums and psychics rely on interpretation, some people assume that if a medium isn't accurate 100% of the time, then that means they're a fraud. Perhaps it wouldn't surprise you that the number one fear that my clients voice to me is this: "If I charge and I'm wrong, what if people think I'm a fraud?" It's no wonder, huh?

Challenge yourself to be able to give high-quality readings consistently—more than 90% of the time. Challenge yourself to understand, with precision, how your mediumship works so that your interpretation of evidence is spot on 90% of the time, or more! Know also that professionals in every industry are never accurate 100% of the time and that you deserve to be compensated for your very important and impactful work.

Educate your sitter, as I do, before their reading about how you work and how the practice of mediumship works so they feel informed and empowered about the process. You can do this by addressing the *most* important things that you wish they knew before a reading. For example, I always explain that mediums are interpreters more than anything, and that most sitters don't really understand this. I also let them know not to do what we call, "feeding the medium" by sharing lots of information beforehand that I might have brought through during the reading. This robs them of their opportunity to hear information that provides proof of consciousness surviving after death of the human body. This is the whole point of mediumship that gives a healing quality and reminds us that we're not alone, and our loved ones aren't gone forever.

Because mediumship should be accessible to everyone, it should be free. Mediumship can be so powerful and life-changing and therefore, it should be accessible to everyone who wants the experience. I agree with this statement.

Here's the thing: there will never be a time when someone cannot get a high-quality reading for free, and/or for a highly accessible price. Spiritualist churches like *The Journey Within* offer free readings to the public during services and often for individuals as well. There is a platform called Very Soul (www.verysoul.com) where people can sign up for free or financially accessible readings with reviewed mediums. There are always mediums who are incredibly talented who are looking to give free readings to get experience. If you've read my book *When Spirits Speak*, you know that I gave 100 free readings as I was developing and that these readings were incredibly valuable to my sitters.

I've heard some mediums complain about and judge others for charging what they view as astronomical prices for celebrities or the wealthy. I remember watching an interview with John Edward where he shared that he didn't enjoy reading for celebrities because of the baggage he said they carry. While I've yet to do it myself, I'd imagine it's a high-pressure situation that requires a significant amount of energy. If charging a higher price is an energetic match for you as a medium, by all means, do it. There most certainly are other mediums, who are as mind-blowingly talented as you are, who are willing to do it for free, or for much less.

I promise you that I will never tell you to charge more than you're comfortable with. Still, you'll have to be willing to crunch some numbers to face the reality of whether or not it's possible to make a living as a medium based on your current rates and the offers you have in place. If you have the dream of this being your profession you've got to be willing to find a financially sustainable way to do it. That means that your needs are fully met. If not, it's unlikely that it will be enjoyable and fulfilling for the long term, and sadly, you'll be of much less use to the people who need you most.

MISTAKE #3: FAILING TO CREATE A BUSINESS MODEL THAT PROVIDES THE PATHWAY TO PROFITABILITY

Because so many spiritual practitioners trade dollars for hours and don't usually have offers that allow them to leverage their business, they fail to create a business model that provides a pathway to profitability. Instead, as we've discussed previously, their business model consists of offers that leave them in a scarcity mindset because they are scrounging to book as many one-on-one sessions as possible.

Even if they do book lots of one-on-one sessions, they ultimately hit burnout, right? But there's something else just as important to keep in mind. Many entrepreneurs who start booking clients cannot create the pathway to profitability because they spend the majority of their time, or almost all of it, working *in* their business. Working *in* your business means working *with* clients. For example, when you're giving readings you're working *with* clients. When you're hosting a training or workshop, you're working *with* clients.

What about the time every business owner needs to be planning, marketing, and looking ahead in terms of new projects and the growth of their business? Those things are things you focus on when you're working *on* your business. Without that time to work on your business you can be just as stuck in a hamster wheel of burnout as you might be by only offering one-on-one, dollar per hour, services. Unfortunately, trading dollars for hours and spending too much time working in your business go hand and hand. Both are usually happening when entrepreneurs are struggling to make a living.

I'll caution you right from the start, that whatever business model you feel most pulled to design should allow you to be working with clients about 40% of the time, leaving the other 60% of your time to be spent working *on* your business. This so-very-important guideline ties into the long-term sustainability of your business, and not just financially, but energetically, creatively, efficiency, and fulfillment-wise!

Here are examples of some of the offers in my business model that allow me to leverage my business and create long-term sustainability on all levels. First, remember that I do offer one-on-one mediumistic readings and spiritual assessments, but that they do *not* help me leverage because these offers are trading dollars for hours. However, giving these readings are important because they keep me sharp in my craft, and they also help me display my work to my audience. What they don't provide is an ability to leverage my business and my resources of energy, time, money, and creativity.

So how do I leverage my business? How does my business model work? I leverage my business with offers like my *Mediumship Development Circle*, my *Speaking with Spirits* course, and my *Profitable Spiritual Medium* mentorship program. These are all powerful ways for me to serve many, but *still* honor the sustainability feature of my business in every way that I've discussed. I have far more clients than if I were to only work by offering one-on-one sessions/readings. I also have far more time and energy to be working on my business and doing other things I love, like spending time with my family and friends.

CHAPTER 4

WHAT TO DO INSTEAD TO MAKE A LIVING AS A MEDIUM

I've shared with you the top three mistakes to avoid when you're growing your business as a medium. Now you might be thinking, "Ok Mel, but what should I be doing instead?" I'm excited to tell you what I've done to avoid these mistakes and create even the simplest of business models that allow me to leverage, and create a profit sooner in my business. I'll be sharing what my business model looked like the first 18 months after I started working professionally, the number one thing *more* people should be doing when they market to attract the *right* clients, and more!

1) DISPLAY YOUR WORK AND KNOWLEDGE TO THE RIGHT PEOPLE.

There are two critical mistakes entrepreneurs make, whether just starting out or already established but struggling. The first is that they aren't marketing in a way that makes it clear *who* they are trying to attract and what *problem* they are trying to solve. Many times it's because they haven't defined their ideal client and are still learning what their ideal clients' struggles and desires are. This leads to marketing that is too general or inconsistent.

The other mistake is that they market themselves in a way that fails to *engage* their client. It's one thing to share information with your ideal clients that you think they want to know. Sometimes, this can be effective to a certain extent, but consumers today expect more. They expect to be wowed in order to get their attention. They want fast and effective answers to their questions and solutions for their problems. This is why it is so important to *show* your clients what you have to offer instead of *telling* them. We want to *display* our work to the *right* people so they can *feel* and *experience* what it would be like to work with us, and then engage them by giving them easy ways to say yes to spending more time with us, even if it's free to begin. I'll give examples shortly.

First let's talk about being clear in terms of *who* your ideal client is and the problem that you're trying to solve for them. It's always the first step. Until you fully understand these details, you won't have a profitable business. I help my clients with this first step by teaching them to identify what I call the 3 P's for their ideal client.

The first P is for *person*. Who *is* this person that you're looking to attract? For me, my P is someone who has lost a loved one and desires to connect with them through a medium and develop their own mediumistic skills so they can find peace and help others to do the same.

The second P is for *pain*. What is the pain point(s) that this person is experiencing? It could be that they have lost a loved one and may still be grieving that loss. Maybe they miss feeling connected to that loved one or they don't feel as spiritually connected to themselves. Maybe they don't feel they have command over their spiritual skills or they feel they are experiencing a spiritual awakening but they don't know how to understand the spiritual aspect of themselves. Maybe they are afraid or nervous to pursue their mediumship or are afraid of calling themselves a medium even though they feel strongly pulled to that path.

The third P is for *pleasure*. What are their strong desires that would bring them pleasure and fulfillment? They want to connect with those they've lost through a medium. They want to feel more connected to their loved one(s) on the other side always, or more often. They want to better understand the spiritual aspect of themselves. They want to speak with, and be guided by, someone who understands the spiritual awakening they are going through. They want to be in a community with like-minded people who can discuss mediumship and spirituality. They want to develop their skills as a medium. They want to have a greater understanding of how mediumship works.

Many successful businesses create what's called a client avatar. This client avatar is who they market their business to. If they are always speaking to this specific person, it helps them stay consistent, and tailor their messages. I have a client avatar named Megan. Megan lost her sister and that loss was the main event that sparked her mediumship journey and allowed her to become aware of her mediumistic skills.

Once you've identified an ideal client, or avatar, you want everything that you share about your work to speak directly to this person. But, speaking to the person isn't enough. You also have to speak to their pain points and pleasure points. People are busy. The honest truth is that nobody is going to donate their precious time to listen to you talk about your work until they feel you're speaking directly to them and answering their most burning questions and presenting solutions to their most painful problems.

We'll dive into this more deeply in part two of this book. For now, start thinking about a specific person, who you know personally or know of, who feels like an absolutely ideal client for you. In chapter five, you'll more clearly define your client avatar and create a 3-P statement about exactly who you work with, as well as their pain points and pleasure points. For now, you can start by listing all of the details you can think of for each of their Ps.

Person	Pain	Pleasure

Once you've got a solid grasp on the 3 Ps for your ideal client, it's time to start *displaying* your work to them so they can *feel* and *experience* what it would be like to work with you. How do you do that?

First, you must have an idea of how you can help your ideal clients. For me, I can give readings as a medium to help them connect to their loved ones. I can give them a spiritual assessment to help give them clarity and validate their spiritual abilities. I can offer them my book, my course, and my mediumship development circle to help them develop their skills as a medium. If this is how I can help my clients with paid offers, I can now begin thinking of ways to help them get a feel for my work and what it might be like to work with me, even before they've said yes to a paid offer.

What would be a good way to display my work and give my followers an experience if I want them to invest in a mediumship reading? I record my mediumship readings and when I get permission, I share them online so people can get a feel for the style of my mediumship and the effect it has on my sitter. This makes my work more of an experience for them because more often than not, I'm showing them what I do instead of telling them. I also prompt them with a question about the reading they watched so that a conversation about mediumship can get started and my ideal client can engage with me.

If I want a prospective client to invest in a spiritual assessment, I'll post recordings of my spiritual assessments that I've given. If I want them to think about enrolling in my courses or development circles, I'll create content videos that answer their most burning questions about mediumship and showcase my skills as a teacher. When followers watch a how-to video of mine, they can imagine what it might be like to learn from me in my course or development circle. While these aren't the only ways to display your work and give your audience more of an experience as you market, they are a few examples that might get you thinking about creative ways to showcase your work to your audience.

2) CREATE A BUSINESS MODEL THAT'S SUSTAINABLE AND PROVIDES A PATHWAY TO PROFITABILITY.

It might not surprise you that one of the things to do *instead*, is to create a business model that *is* sustainable and can lead you to actually making enough money to live comfortably. But how?

When you're first starting out, you don't want to spread yourself too thin by offering a multitude of different services or products that have yet to be validated as compelling offers by your ideal clients. What's more, you don't want to confuse your potential client. Have you ever heard the phrase, "the confused customer doesn't buy"? It's true. If you have a handful of different offerings, a potential client may hem and haw about which they should choose. This happens especially if the offers aren't differentiated enough.

Remember that you don't have an unlimited runway for takeoff when it comes to putting something out there and validating that it's actually something the people that you want to attract, want! I strongly suggest keeping what you have to offer straightforward and simple. For mediums, it's not that complicated to know that our customers want to connect with their loved ones who have passed away. With this in mind, here is what I tell my clients to focus on with their offers to begin creating their pathway to profitability.

When Just Starting:

- One offer that helps you stay relevant, sharpen your craft and expertise, and is low-cost in terms of resources required.
- One offer that can become a cash cow, help you leverage, and is low-cost in terms of resources required.

For the Future (Once Your Initial Offers are Validated):

- One offer that has the potential to be a **major** cash cow, create massive leverage, and is low to high-cost in terms of resources required.
- One offer that has the potential to create more passive income, and is low to high-cost in terms of resources required. *(Optional)*

I'm about to share a juicy list of all kinds of offers that you might think about as a part of your business model. Before we get into that though, you've got to understand the difference between a low, medium, and high-cost offer in terms of resources required. I'm not talking about the price of your offer. I'm talking about how much it's going to cost *you* to create and deliver these offers in terms of your time, money, and energy.

Recall how I gave the example of an entrepreneur creating a course when they're first starting out that no one signs up for. While there are many reasons that this can happen—including not understanding who your ideal client is, not having created an audience, etc.—one of the reasons I don't suggest this as your first move is that a course is a high-cost offer.

- It costs a considerable amount of *energy* to conduct ideal client interviews, create the content and organize it in a way that gets your clients results, market it, deliver the course, and take on the customer support aspect.
- It costs a considerable amount of *money* to host your course, set up the back end logic, write and design a sales page, create order forms, edit and design your content, and market your course.
- You can likely understand why the resource of *time* is high-cost for a course. If you were to hire team members,

that would lessen the time cost, but it would definitely increase the money cost.

Now let's compare this high-cost course offer to a low-cost offer. A one-on-one reading is a low-cost offer. Why is that? While it can take a bit of energy and time to book your first paying client, it's a hell of a lot less effort than everything that goes into creating, marketing, and selling out a course. For many mediums, after they've reached a certain level of proficiency by reading for free, they're surprised how easy it is to book a paid reading simply from referrals. There is little to no preparation that must be done before giving a reading. This is not the same for a course. While it takes time and energy to deliver a reading, it still requires a much lower cost in terms of your resources when all is said and done.

To put it simply, a low-cost offer costs the least in terms of time, money, and energy. A high-cost offer is the opposite. The problem is that new business owners don't always have the experience or foresight when it comes to how much the creation of new offers might cost them. By the time they figure out that an initial offer was too high-cost, it's too late and they're burnt out or feeling overwhelmed and hopeless.

Let's look at a list of different offers you might be interested in providing as a medium and I'll share examples of why each offer is low, medium, or high-cost. By no means is this an exhaustive list, but it'll help you get your mind going. I'll go deeper into why I recommend these one to two offers when you're first starting out versus the next one or two that you might add once you've validated your initial offers and are generating dependable revenue from them.

EXAMPLES OF OFFERS

One-On-One Readings *(Intuitive/Mediumistic) Low-Cost*

While one-on-one readings do require you to trade dollars for hours, they have many benefits. They help you stay relevant and continue to sharpen your craft and expertise. They are also low-cost. The time, energy, and money that it takes to market and deliver this type of offer is relatively low.

Spiritual Assessments *Low-Cost*

Spiritual Assessments are another type of one-on-one reading/offer so the same benefits and energy investment as one-on-one readings apply.

Private Coaching *Low-Cost*

While private coaching uses a different skillset than working professionally as a medium and giving readings, it sharpens your craft and expertise in a different but valuable way. It also trades dollars for hours, but is low-cost in terms of your time, money, and energy.

Small Group Mediumship/Psychic Coaching *Low-Cost*

Small group coaching is a good way to add some leverage to your business! I constantly have students asking me for private coaching. I don't offer it because I don't want more dollars-for-hours offers. Additionally, private coaching is something I did for many years in my previous online marketing business and I've hit my fulfillment quota.

What I do enjoy is offering small group mediumship coaching. Usually I add it as a bonus for those who enroll early in my development circle or courses, but I'm known to offer it from time to time to my subscriber list as well because mediums are so hungry for this offer and they rave about their experience. I usually have 4-6 mediums in a small group coaching session where I include Q&A time and curated exercises based on the needs of each individual. This offer sharpens your craft and expertise as well as your abilities as a teacher, and it's low-cost in terms of time, money, and energy.

Group Readings *Low-Med Cost*

Group readings can be an amazing way to add leverage to your business. When you conduct a group reading, you're still continuing to stay relevant with your craft and you're sharpening your skills, but you're no longer trading dollars for hours. In a group reading you can serve many people at once. A group reading is pretty low-cost in terms of time, but can be slightly higher-cost in terms of energy and money. This is because reading for a group and bringing through multiple spirits will require more energy. It will also require more marketing efforts to get multiple people at a reading instead of just one person. With just a couple hundred people on my list and following me on social media I was able to sell out four group readings a year with 15 people at each reading, paying $35 per person. That's a total of $2,100 a year from group readings, which isn't much. It's likely I could have offered more group readings for a larger audience, but what's most important is to look at what's possible in terms of this leveraged offer, once you have a much larger following. There is a famous medium I admire who offers about two virtual group readings a month and charges about $20 per attendee. While I don't know for sure, I've heard rumors that they allow 800 people to register for each virtual group reading. Based on their YouTube following of about 500,000 followers, getting 800 attendees per group reading is easily feasible. If we do the math, that's $16,000 per group reading, which lasts about 90 minutes. This is an example of pretty incredible leverage. Of course, growing a following of half a million people takes time, but that doesn't mean you can't start where you are!

Development Circles *Low-Med Cost*

Development circles are a wonderful way to leverage your business if you feel pulled to add a teaching aspect to your work. I am a natural born teacher so development circles are one of my favorite offers in my business. The reason development circles are low to medium cost is because unlike a course, you don't need to create a large body of content with modules or worksheets, have your content edited and designed, and then pay for a hosting platform.

A development circle only requires you to have a space to teach. I work virtually so I use Zoom which is a world more affordable than a platform where you host a course and provide a forum for students. This makes a development circle low-cost in terms of money. It's also low to medium cost in terms of energy because it takes me about two hours a week to teach a class and about 20 minutes a week to prepare for my classes. This means it's not taking a large percentage of my overall time working during the week.

In terms of the time and energy cost to market a circle, I'd put it in the medium category. It's always more work to have multiple people sign up for an offer versus just one person. Whether it falls into the low or medium energy cost bracket for marketing depends on how large your audience is and how ideal your clients are, as well as how much trust you've built with them. Even in my first year offering a development circle, my circles provided an average of $20,000 - $25,000 a quarter in revenue once I had three different circles that sold out with between 12-14 students in each circle.

Workshops/Trainings/Retreats *Med - High Cost*

When it comes to workshops, trainings, and retreats, let's first talk about the versions of these that are paid and in person. A lot of entrepreneurs get excited about the idea of offering a live in-person workshop, training, or retreat. While it's possible to do this on the "cheap" if your event is local, you have local followers, and you've got a great deal that's either free or very affordable in terms of a physical space to host, these types of events are often high-cost and low profit. I have a friend who started a new business and rented a space for her first event. She told me it was "way too expensive" and left her in the red. I will say that it was her first event and she wanted it to feel elevated, but my larger point is that this is a very common experience.

When I launched my first book, I decided to do a live event where I read from the book and conducted an in-person group reading. It was a great event and my goal was *not* for it to be a money making event. While we sold out of all of the books, the books are not expensive offers. The event cost $2,300 and it was not profitable. That's a cost that's easy to absorb for me financially at this point in my business, so it was a great choice to have the event for other reasons. We got lots of great video footage and professional pictures that I can use for marketing purposes and to build credibility. However, if I was just starting out and I hadn't validated any offers, it'd be a much larger cost to absorb.

Early on in my entrepreneurial journey, back in 2014, I hosted a retreat with a dear friend of mine. The cost of time, energy, and money was extremely high. I remember us meeting multiple times a week for at least a few months. We spent many hours planning and the energy was beyond just about anything I'd done at that point. It was a great learning experience and served many other important purposes for us as young entrepreneurs, but our profitability from that event was extremely low, about $3,000 a person.

At this point in my entrepreneurial career, I've hosted larger events – investing between $50,000-$60,000—to get 150-200 butts in seats and then creating revenues over a three day event around $600,000-$750,000. However, I didn't get to that point early on in my career. It turned out to be a much smarter move to validate my two simple offers to start and then, as I learned more about marketing and how to speak to and support my ideal client, these bigger endeavors became easier and more profitable.

I share these stories to show you just how high-cost in-person events tend to be in terms of time, energy, and money. For highly experienced entrepreneurs who know their ideal client and their offers well, who have a sizable following, who are great marketers, who have a team, and who make offers from these live events, they can be a powerful aspect of your business. When you're just starting out, I do *not* recommend starting here.

There is also an aspect of workshops and trainings that can be offered online for free. They typically serve as a platform for making an offer to your audience and can be very effective. Perhaps you've attended a free training, workshop, or webinar, and at the end you've been offered something pretty compelling that is the perfect extension of a great free experience. These options are still medium to high-cost. They require knowledge and considerable skill to create content and an experience for your ideal client that leaves them hungry for your paid offer. They also require an audience large enough to have many people register for your free training. From that free training, only a small percentage of them may actually say yes to your paid offer.

Courses (Live and Automated/Self-Study) *High-Cost*

At the beginning of 2025 I was talking to my husband about my goals for my business. I told him, "This is going to be a great year, but an expensive one."

"Why is that?" he asked.

"I'm creating and offering two courses this year, and you know how expensive that can be."

It took me back to 2017, when I created two courses and enrolled clients in three in my online marketing business! It was a busy year.

You recall what I've already shared with you about the high cost of creating a course.

- It costs a considerable amount of *energy* to conduct ideal client interviews, create the content and organize it in a way that gets your clients results, market it, and deliver the course and take on the customer support aspect.
- It costs a considerable amount of *money* to host your course, set up the back-end logic, write and design a sales page, create order forms, edit and design your content, and market your course.
- You can likely understand why the resource of *time*—after I've listed the above costs—is high-cost for a course. If you were to hire team members that would lessen the time cost, but it would definitely increase the money cost.

It's important to acknowledge that with new advances in technology, like artificial intelligence, creating content and organizing it, as well as writing sales pages, sales emails, and handling customer support is becoming faster and easier than ever before. That means that the cost to create a course is lessening. Still, learning to use AI ethically, and in a way that is simply an extension of your own unique brand identity and ideas, takes time. It would be difficult to have AI substitute for the knowledge, know-how, and creativity that is required of an entrepreneur to create an effective and compelling course and a financially successful launch right out of the gates as a new entrepreneur. I never use AI to do the creative aspect of my work. There are too many disadvantages like stunting your creative mind and your growth process that is a byproduct of coming up with your own ideas.

Books, Spiritual Decks, Products, etc. *High-Cost*

While books, spiritual decks, and products are created and marketed differently, I group them together because they are all products that you can hold in your hand. All other offers that I've listed are services that people experience with you in real time.

These offers are much lower price points than many of the services that were previously shared. That means that in order to create a sustainable income from them, you'd have to sell quite a lot. For example, you'd need to sell 2,000, $25 dollar books to create $50,000 in revenue. If you were going to use another platform to print, sell, and package your book, deck, or product, you'd receive only 35% - 70% of that revenue. Books and spiritual decks require writing and content creation and sometimes illustration work that demands lots of energy and time. There is also editing and design. For all of these products, the packaging, printing, and delivery are large tasks that are an expense of money, time, and energy if done on your own.

I suggest these offers as something supplemental and also a step along your ideal client's journey to saying yes to another validated offer, like a course or development circle that is leveraged. While some people write books or decks or create products that then turn into more expansive businesses, generally it's wise to expend less of your time, money, and energy until you have validated your first two offers, making sure one of them has the potential to provide leverage on all fronts. This is so that when you publish your book and put out your deck, that your clients have somewhere to go to continue working with you. That's when the work you've done on your product, book, or deck can really pay off.

Designing Offers That Create a Client Pathway

Keep in mind that businesses that create a pathway to profitability have also created what I call a client pathway. To explain to you what a client pathway is, imagine your client becoming aware of you and then going on a journey of yeses. Some of those yeses will be free. For example, they say yes to watching a video reel that you've published online. Perhaps that leads them to say yes to subscribing to your email. Maybe then they say yes by opening an email that you send out. After that, they might say their first paid yes by registering for a group reading that you're hosting for a nominal amount. After a group reading they may decide they want to say yes to a private mediumship reading for $250. Or perhaps they are more interested in learning from you so they say their next yes to your development circle for $555. Do you see why I call this designing a client pathway? A client pathway should seamlessly anticipate their next desire that you can fulfill with your following offers.

Another way to understand the client pathway is to imagine a three story building where as the yeses accumulate, your ideal client goes up the escalator to the next floor. If you look at the image below, you'll see that the bottom level is labeled "Free Easy Yeses."

These are the initial ways for new potential clients to say yes to engaging with you. Potential clients generally need several interactions—anywhere between 7 and 50!—with your brand before they are willing to say yes to a paid offer. This is why it is so important to have several options for potential clients to experience you in a way that is not initially asking them to invest. Below I've listed a handful of ways that clients can say a free, easy yes.

CLIENT PATHWAY PYRAMID

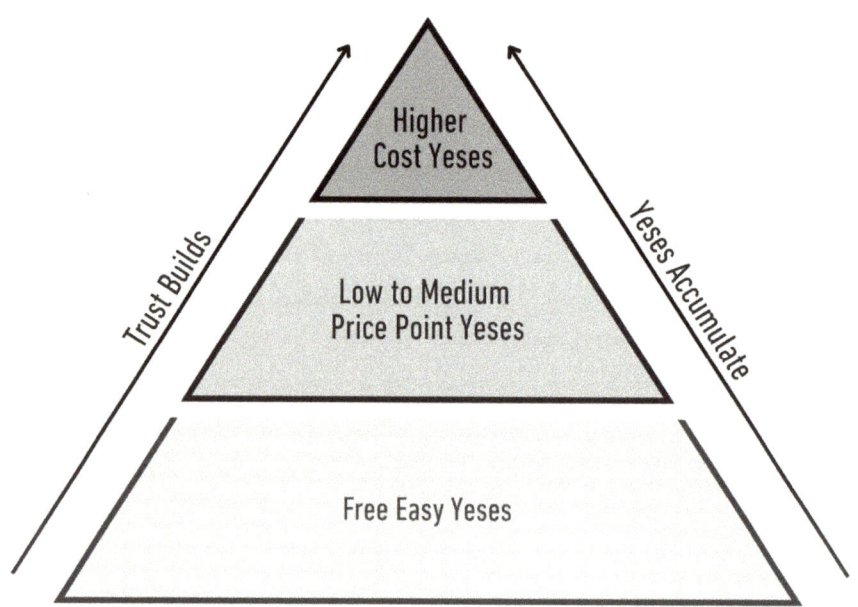

Free Easy Yeses

- Watch an online video
- Like an online post
- Comment on online content
- Follow you online
- Check out your website
- Private message you online or send you an email
- Download a free offer
- Subscribe to your list
- Open your email

- Respond to an email
- Click on a link in your email

CLIENT PATHWAY PYRAMID

Free Easy Yeses

— Subscribe to your list   Like a post —

— Comment on online content   Follow you online —

— Responding to your email   Downloading a free offer —

— Watch online video   Opening your email and reading it —

The next level on the pyramid is the low to medium price point yeses. Once your ideal client has engaged with you in an easy and free way, a percentage of them will be willing to take the escalator to the next level by saying yes to a paid offer. The most important thing about this next step in your client pathway is that the Free Easy Yes offers seamlessly lead to the paid offers. You might be surprised to learn how often entrepreneurs get this wrong. Let's say you have a free downloadable piece of content that is called, "5 ways to use crystals to calm your anxiety." While you might think that will attract the kind of person who is interested in mediumship, it's still not seamlessly aligned with your next paid offer if your next paid offer is a mediumship reading. Just because someone is interested in crystals doesn't mean they're interested in getting a reading or becoming a medium.

On my YouTube channel, I share recordings of my mediumship readings and my spiritual assessments when I have permission from my sitters. This means that a free and easy way to engage with me online is to watch those videos. My following low to medium price point yeses are... can you guess? A spiritual assessment reading or a mediumship reading. My free content that someone can download is, "3 easy exercises to strengthen your clairs and speak to Spirit." Someone who is looking to strengthen their mediumistic skills, or even their psychic skills, would be interested in this free download. A low to medium price point yes that follows that free download is my mediumship development circle. Do you see how those free and easy ways of engaging with me align precisely with my low to medium price point yeses? Here are some examples of low to medium price point yeses.

Low to Medium Price Point Yeses

- Group Reading
- Online Training/Workshop
- Spiritual Assessment
- Mediumistic Reading
- Psychic Reading
- Small-Group Coaching
- Private Coaching
- Mediumship Development Circle *(This may be considered a medium price point yes to some or a higher price point yes to others so it is optional to include it here.)*
- Self-Study Course *(This may be considered a medium price point yes to some or a higher price point yes to others so it is optional to include it here.)*

- Book
- Spiritual Deck

CLIENT PATHWAY PYRAMID

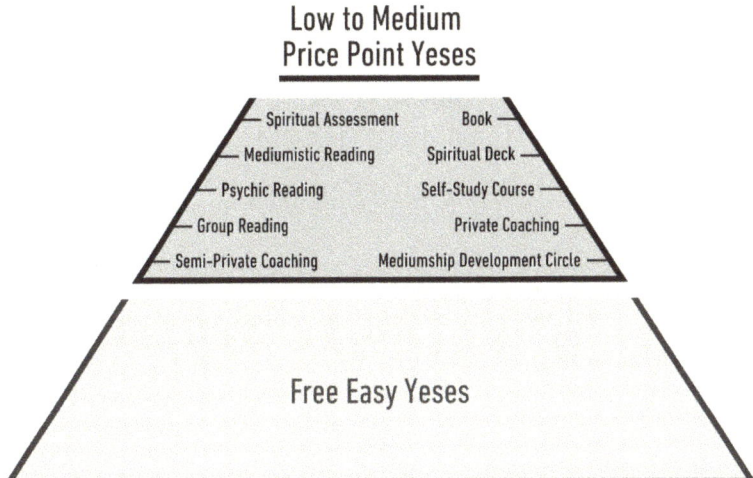

Low to Medium Price Point Yeses

— Spiritual Assessment — Book —
— Mediumistic Reading — Spiritual Deck —
— Psychic Reading — Self-Study Course —
— Group Reading — Private Coaching —
— Semi-Private Coaching — Mediumship Development Circle —

Free Easy Yeses

The final level of the pyramid would be your higher price point yeses. Just as it is important that your easy yeses transition seamlessly into your low to medium price point yeses, your low to medium price point yeses should seamlessly transition to your higher price point yeses. While some of my clients come to me only because they are grieving the loss of a loved one and want a reading, others come for that reason but also because they want to develop as a medium. They might book a spiritual assessment and/or a mediumistic reading and then also want to join my mediumship course or development circle, or both. It's proven to me that my clients move along the client pathway that I've created with ease and that as the trust builds, they continue to invest and move themselves up the pyramid. Many of them invest repeatedly in my low to medium price point offers and my high price point offers for continued mentorship. Here is a short list of high price point offers.

High Price Point Yeses

- Self-Study Course *(This may be considered a medium price point yes to some or a higher price point yes to others so it is optional to include it here.)*
- Mediumship Development Circle *(This may be considered a medium price point yes to some or a higher price point yes to others so it is optional to include it here.)*
- Live Course/Mentorship Program
- In-Person Retreat

CLIENT PATHWAY PYRAMID

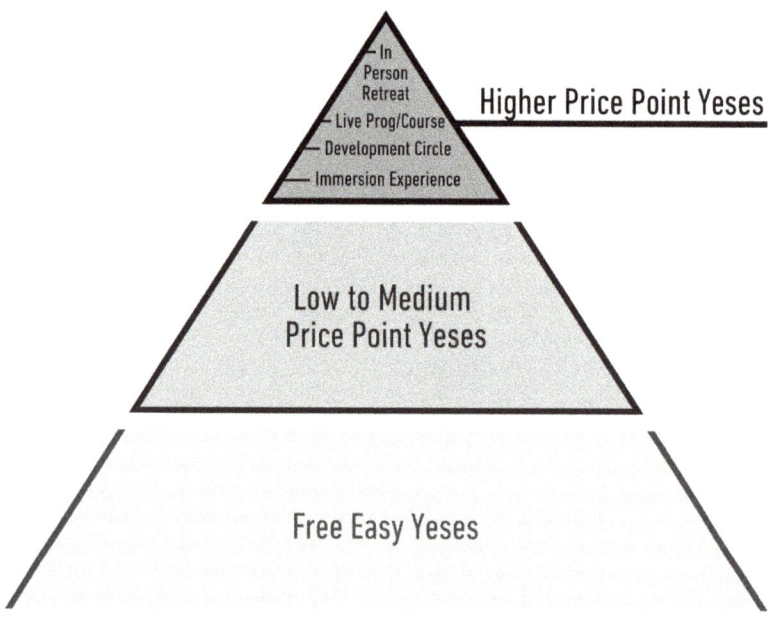

Now let's revisit what I initially shared with you about the offers I recommend when you're just starting out.

When Just Starting:

- One offer that helps you stay relevant, sharpen your craft and expertise, and is low-cost in terms of resources required.
- One offer that can become a cash cow, help you leverage, and is low-cost in terms of resources required.

I'd like to show you how I follow my own advice in my current mediumship business. When I was just starting out, mediumship readings were a low-cost offer that helped me stay relevant and sharpen my craft and expertise. This was the only thing that I put out when I was beginning. I had previously set a goal to give 100 readings for free and I made it into the 70s before I was getting so many inquiries, and feeling confident enough, that I simply had to start charging to make my work sustainable. About six months later, when that first offer was validated and I was consistently selling out every appointment available for mediumship readings, I decided to open enrollment for my own mediumship development circle. My mediumship development circle was my cash cow offer that helped me leverage and was still low-cost. With these two offers alone, I can generate $120,000/year by giving three readings a week and hosting three circles with a total of ~42 students, four times a year.

As my business got to the point where my two starting out offers were validated, I began to add more offers that were medium to high-cost in terms of resources required.

For the Future (Once Your Initial Offers are Validated):

- One offer that has the potential to be a **major** cash cow, create massive leverage, and is low to high-cost in terms of resources required.
- One offer that has the potential to create more passive income, and is low to high-cost in terms of resources required. *(Optional)*

My course, *Speaking With Spirits*, and my mentorship program, *The Profitable Spiritual Medium* are my offers that have the potential to be major cash cows, create massive leverage, and are low to high-cost in terms of resources required. *Speaking With Spirits* is a four-month, live program that walks you through the A - Z of everything I wish I'd known about mediumship as I entered my spiritual awakening and felt called to this work. One of the big differences between this course and my mediumship development circles is the defined course content that covers the A - Z of mediumship and can't fit into the format of a development circle.

The nuanced details of mediumship and step-by-step education is easily presented in this live program format whereas a development circle is much less formal and focuses on creating a space to practice *without* recorded lessons and highly detailed written content. In addition, there is a user friendly online forum, weekly homework, and live Q&A/practice calls each week. *The Profitable Spiritual Medium* mentorship program is designed specifically for mediums who want to create financially sustainable businesses so they can earn a living doing this work. In fact, the tagline is, *how to make six figures and beyond talking to dead people*.

Both of these offers allow me to work with more clients than when I only had readings and development circles available as offers. My readings and development circles sold out every quarter and there was no room for me to continue to increase my income and impact without creating them. I can serve more students in my course and mentorship program than I can in my development circles.

My second "for the future" offer that is optional, has the potential to create passive income, and is low to high-cost, is something I did right from the start when I discovered my mediumistic abilities. As soon as I decided to give 100 readings for free, I started my YouTube channel, Mediumship With Mel.

It was strange how it happened. Back when I was working as an online marketing strategist, I'd purchased a YouTube course in 2019 that I never ended up putting to use. This was unlike me. I have never been a procrastinator or the least bit unmotivated. In January of 2022, when I studied for the first time at Arthur Findlay College, I got a spiritual assessment from an amazing medium named Anne-Marie Bond. I loved her from the first moment I saw her. During the weekly courses, you can choose a mentor that you'd like to have a reading from. I knew instantly that I would choose Anne-Marie and that I wanted a spiritual assessment from her. To this day, that assessment was by far the most powerful one that I've received, and I've had a handful of them. Anne-Marie said many things that gave me powerful validation as a medium and she was spot on. At the end of the spiritual assessment, she told me that I needed to start a YouTube channel as soon as I got home. She said it was strange because she'd never gotten that before. I still have the recording that I've listened to many times. "You're going to need it. You're going to need it," she says. "People are going to want to see you work and invite you to speak and read on stages."

I started the course and got my YouTube channel up and running right away when I got home. Keep in mind that as a previous online marketing strategist, I had a knack for marketing and that's what made it easier for me to get things going quickly. If I had never run a business before, I'd have to read this book first—especially part two where I'll be sharing my Client Attraction Framework. It explains how to spend your time on a daily and weekly basis to make sure that you're taking client-attracting actions.

While I knew that my YouTube channel would likely be a slow burn in terms of creating any passive income, I knew it was possible. In the meantime, I thought it was a great way to create an audience without paying for advertising. In my mind, the sooner you start, the better. As I write this book in 2025, my monetized YouTube channel brings in less than $600 annually. However, my revenue will continue to grow with my subscriber count.

I make a revenue stream like this optional because it's time-consuming to create and can distract you from solidifying the basics like understanding who your ideal client is, how to speak to them, what you'll offer them, and how to validate the offer(s).

The most important things to keep in mind when it comes to creating a pathway to profitability are: 1) the two kinds of offers to make when you're just starting and getting them validated as soon as possible, *and* 2) making sure that there are seamless transitions along your client pathway from one offer to the next.

3) YOU MUST GENERATE TRAFFIC—START BUILDING A FOLLOWING TODAY!

I was teaching a 90-minute business workshop to some mediums in my mediumship development circle. It focused on creating a 90-day profit plan. In one section of the profit plan, I had my clients work backward, first deciding the amount of revenue they wanted to bring in over the following quarter and then what offers they would create to generate that revenue.

I had a student who had an ambitious plan to offer group readings each week. She was crunching her numbers with the assumption that she'd sell out all her group readings with 15 people attending each. I asked her how many followers or subscribers she currently had. She said she didn't have any. While her plan was good in many ways, she still needed to decide how she was going to start building the kind of following that would support sold out weekly group readings.

While it's a great start to have created a client pathway that seamlessly leads from one offer to another, getting those free, easy yeses requires an audience of people who know about you, like you, and trust you! In fact, once you have clarity about who your ideal client is and the problem that you're helping them solve, it's *never* too soon to start building your audience.

We'll discuss more of the strategy behind creating an audience in part two of this book. For now, I'll share some examples of the different avenues I've taken, and a friend of mine has taken, to create an audience. That being said, understand that this book is *not* about becoming a social media expert on any platform(s). Platforms come and go so it's paramount for a larger bird's eye strategy about *how* to engage with your audience in a way that builds trust and rapport. New entrepreneurs will fixate on questions like, "How often should I post?" I promise you that it's more important to learn how to show up with potential clients in a way that allows them to *experience* you and understand what it might be like to work with you. This is the skill that will go much farther in creating a following and outlive any platform over time.

The good news is, there isn't just one way to do it. I have students who tell me how much they despise being online and I can tell you that as a former online marketing strategist for over eight years during an extremely divisive period in America, I often feel the same. Negative comments, trolling, and misinformation can be a hard thing to take. Add in the fact that so many mediums are extremely empathic and the online world can be a major energy suck and downer.

When I decided to create a business as a medium, I channeled my experience building audiences through online marketing strategies. Having this background laid the groundwork for a new model that would work better for who I'd become and where I was in my life. As a mother of two young children, and someone who enjoys being present in my life, I am not available to be constantly tied to electronics and the online world.

As I share more in this chapter and in part two of this book, think about what might be the most effective way for *you* to stop being a best-kept secret and to start allowing people to learn about your work. Just because you hear impressive stories about a person creating a following one way doesn't mean it has to be yours if it doesn't feel good to you. You'll see shortly that my medium bestie markets her mediumship business on TikTok. I'm so happy that she's been able to attract clients from that platform, but in all honesty, you couldn't pay me *any* amount of money to join TikTok. I'm not interested in consuming or creating short form content and I can't stand feeling beholden to my phone or social media. That being said, AI can take a lot of the work out of social media so that you have more online freedom.

I remember hosting a business training with my mediumship students and one of them saying to me, "I'm not really a fan of social media, but I feel like I have to do it." I asked her what her aspirations were for her mediumship business. She said she wanted to be able to book readings consistently. I told her that getting clients via referral was a super powerful way to get booked in the mediumship industry and that she should start there if that's what felt best.

Here's what felt best to me when I began creating my mediumship business.

MY WAY OF CREATING AN AUDIENCE

1) YouTube

It's a great trust builder.

People decide to become followers when they trust you, like you, and know you. If you provide excellent content that is helpful to them, and you display the quality of your work well, that trust builds. YouTube is one of the only long-form video content platforms. People come to watch your videos for longer than just a few seconds. That means that if they like your videos, they'll watch lots of them and the trust can build *very* quickly. In addition, because video content builds trust much faster than written content, it's powerful for turning subscribers into paying clients.

I control my own online schedule.

YouTube allows me to work on my schedule. I don't have to worry about posting multiple times a day or generating content every single day. When I began my channel, I went on the platform about four times a week. Now the *only* way I engage with the platform is by posting a new video once a week. It's true that if I was on YouTube daily, or if I released more videos, I could likely grow my audience even faster, but I don't need to. For me, slow and steady wins the race and once I hit 1,500 subscribers, I was able to easily create a 6-figure a year plus business.

Remember as well that I'm prolific when it comes to content creation and I enjoy being on camera. That makes YouTube the perfect platform for me. Before I became pregnant with my second daughter, I cranked videos out at a rate of nearly five a week and created a year and a half's worth of content ahead of time. I enjoyed this because it was all on my schedule and I can get ahead with videos and then have very little that I need to do for upkeep.

This attraction platform provides continuity.

While YouTube does require you to be engaged on the platform, especially when you're just starting your channel, once you do the work to create new content, that content lives forever and continues to work for you for free! Every viewer of your video helps YouTube understand who your ideal client is and then YouTube feeds your videos to more of those kinds of people. For me, nothing could be better! I *love* creating content and presenting it because that is suited to my natural skills. It doesn't feel like hard work. I know that with every video I make, the time I'm putting in now will create something that will work on my behalf for as long as that video is online.

It effectively displays the quality of my work.

Remember, it's paramount to display your work and knowledge to the *right* people so they can *feel* what it would be like to work with you. On YouTube, it's very easy for me to do this by sharing recordings of my readings. This helps potential clients see the quality of my readings and how I interact with my sitters. It lets them know whether or not I feel like the right medium for them and if I'm good enough at what I do for them to be willing to invest in a reading. I also create how-to content videos answering the questions I'm asked most often on my social media accounts or via email. If I don't have comments on my accounts or receive emails, I simply go to the online profiles of other mediums and see what comments they are receiving to get ideas for what content to create. When viewers see how I organize my content and break it down and my style of teaching, they can see whether or not they'd like to take my courses or join a development circle.

It's high-cost initially, low-medium cost long term.

There's no doubt about it, YouTube is a high-cost way to go about building your audience in terms of time and energy. There is most definitely a learning curve and some skills may come easier than others. I'm proficient *enough* with technology that content creation can be a superpower of mine. I also feel comfortable being on video and I'm a good speaker. That means that the high cost of time and energy is worth it for me in the long run. Once I got through the learning curve, I was able to create videos quickly and use them on the YouTube platform with success. That means that my time and energy cost is much lower and easy for me to maintain. If the skills I listed aren't skills that you have, and any one of them feels like pulling teeth, this will likely *not* be the best way for you to grow your audience.

2) Word of Mouth/Referral

Trust transfers

I already shared that people knowing you, liking you, and *trusting* you is key when it comes to getting clients. The thing about clients coming to you via referral or word of mouth is that trust transfers. If you have a friend or family member who you trust and they tell you that I'm a great medium, you're likely to trust me even before we've met. Mediumship is a very personal experience and it can feel vulnerable and private. This is why many people choose a medium who they hear good things about from the people they already know, like, and trust.

Very low-cost

Creating a referral network is definitely low-cost in terms of money. It can also be low-cost in terms of time and energy. A lot of my referrals happen organically by doing my best work when I give readings and teach classes. That's the powerful thing about word of mouth/referrals. If you're excellent at what you do, people can't help but tell their friends and family. Think about it. When you have an amazing experience, what's the first thing that you do? Share about it with someone else!

You can spend more time creating a referral network by reaching out to potential clients on a regular basis in a friendly and non-pushy way, by asking your clients to share your work with others and refer them to you, and by partnering up with other practitioners whose audience overlaps with yours, but who provide an entirely different, but complementary service.

Just know that a referral network does require a high EQ. I have a book coach that I've worked with who is incredible at building genuine relationships with other people and then creating great growth opportunities for both parties. For example, I have therapists who often refer their clients to me when they've lost a loved one. I also refer my students to an energy worker that I see quarterly. If building relationships is a strength of yours, this may be a powerful path to expand your audience.

Not in online jail

When it comes to a referral network, you don't have to create a lot of content, spend a lot of time online, or pay for advertising. That means that you don't have to worry about posting online often or using your brain to think about what you should talk about next. It gives you much more freedom to do things on your own schedule.

3) Instagram

Effectively displays the quality of my work

Like YouTube, Instagram allows me to display the quality of my work to the *right* people so they can *feel* what it would be like to work with me. While I don't share entire recordings of readings, I create short reels to give sneak peeks. I also give sneak peeks of my how-to content videos. These are not as powerful as the longer-form content that I post on YouTube, but they do the job, if only through demonstrating brand consistency across platforms.

Good trust builder

Instagram easily lends itself to video content. That's important because video content allows you to display the quality of your work much more quickly, and often more effectively, than written content. It also allows your audience to feel like they know you much faster than when they read a post. This in turn, builds trust.

Low to medium cost

While I could spend all day on Instagram, for me, it is low-cost because I simply repurpose everything that I've already created on YouTube to Instagram. I also have a rule for myself that I only post two times a week unless I'm incredibly inspired and am having fun creating more content. While this might make an Instagram specialist cringe, it works great for me because it only takes me about 10 minutes a week tops to be engaged at this level.

I mentioned I have a medium bestie. I sat down with her while we were in Essex studying at Arthur Findlay College together. Over dinner, we planned out how she might generate and nurture an audience as a professional medium. Here's what felt best to her.

EMILY'S WAY OF CREATING AN AUDIENCE

1) Instagram

Emily doesn't enjoy creating long-form content.

One of the first things that Emily told me is that, while she doesn't mind being on Instagram, she's not a fan of creating content. She said it doesn't come easily to her and it feels like hard work. I gave her some ideas for doing super short snippets that made Instagram feel more doable for her, and like a good fit.

Displays the quality of her work

I told her that I thought using video to display snippets of her readings and how-to content would be a great way to give her viewers and subscribers more of an experience when they follow her online. I told her what I've shared with you—that it's so important for followers to be able to imagine what it would be like to work with her, instead of just reading a "meh" quote that most people scroll right past in a matter of moments.

Medium cost

Notice how the cost of Instagram is higher for Emily than it is for me. It's important to point out that it will take more or less energy for some people based on their skillset and their audience-building combination to generate their audience using the same platform or strategy. Emily records her readings and edits them primarily for Instagram (and TikTok) so posting her readings takes more work on Instagram than it does for me.

2) TikTok

Displays the quality of her work and can help build trust

For all of the reasons we've discussed above about using video, TikTok allows Emily to display the quality of her work, if only briefly in a post, and builds trust with her audience.

Quick audience growth

While YouTube can be more of a slow burn in terms of growing a large audience, TikTok lends itself to quick audience growth. This is because the algorithm is designed to favor virality. The thing to keep in mind here, is to make sure that your content will *only* be interesting to ideal clients. If you create content simply with the idea of going viral, you'll lower your chances of converting viewers into paid clients.

Low to medium cost

For the same reasons that Instagram is low-cost for me, Emily takes the video that she's already created for Instagram and repurposes it on TikTok. This saves her significant time and energy.

3) Word of Mouth/Referral

Emily also gets lots of business via word of mouth/referral. All of the same pros about a referral network apply in Emily's case too.

- *Trust transfers*
- *Very low-cost*
- *NOT in online jail*

I hope your mind is starting to churn with ideas of what might work for you. There's no limit to the different approaches you might take. This can be overwhelming for some people. I know it was for me when I began my online marketing business back in 2014. Just remember to choose a path that feels sustainable for you so you don't burn out, become resentful, and unable to create a profitable business that makes you happy. We won't make audience building overly complicated. We'll stick to the aspects of generating a following that really make a difference. You can have the largest audience in the world, but if you haven't created a relationship with your followers, you won't have a business.

PART II

THE 5-PART CLIENT ATTRACTION FRAMEWORK

I was sitting in a coffee shop with a dear friend who had been a client of mine back when I was running my business as an online marketing strategist. We had planned to meet and give each other life updates, as usual. I asked her what was new and she was pee-your-pants excited to let me know that she was getting into the world of AI. She had always been great at helping entrepreneurs create systems and processes that kept them organized and helped them create leverage. AI was perfectly aligned with her desire to help entrepreneurs become more efficient and profitable in their businesses. She told me she'd be helping spiritual entrepreneurs use AI to help them scale, save time, and run more profitable businesses. These things were right up my alley and I was interested immediately. Can you tell that she had her 3 Ps for her ideal client down pat?

Her 3 Ps weren't the only thing she had clarity on. She was able to show me an AI bot demonstration that she'd made for another client to give me an idea of what might be possible for me.

While you don't have to meet someone in person at a coffee shop like my friend did to display the quality of your work and help your client experience what you do, the time my friend was spending on client-getting activities paid off for her, even though she'd had no intention of trying to enroll me as a client!

In part two of this book, we're going to get into the nitty gritty of how to spend your time working in and on your business on a daily basis, to actually create some moola while you do what you love. My conversation with my friend was a client-getting activity because she focused on having an engaging conversation that highlighted my pain and pleasure points in my business, helped me have a bite-sized experience with her work, and ultimately led me to saying yes to investing in my business via her support.

During this same conversation, I updated her about my progress writing this very book. I walked her through the outline that I'd mapped out and told her about part two of this book that you're reading now.

"You know how entrepreneurs always start out focusing on the silly stuff that actually wastes all of their time, money, and energy? Like designing their website, or writing a course before they even have any followers who they know are interested in their course."

My friend laughed, "Oh yeah, that was me!"

"That was me too!" I said. "I spent about five years doing a whole lot of non-client getting tasks before I figured it out."

I explained to her that part two of my book would be explaining my 5-Part Client Attraction Framework that I taught when she was a client of mine. We laughed and agreed that focusing on client-getting actions was *the* make or break thing for business owners. It *always* ended up being the deciding factor in terms of whether a business took off or belly flopped.

You'll remember that I was on the strugglebus like no other for quite a while before I got traction and realized that all of my actions were falling into five different categories. If only I had a chance to learn right from the beginning what I'm going to share with you now...

My 5-Part Client Attraction Framework focuses on these categories of client-getting activities:

1) CLARITY

Clarity is about knowing your ideal client along with their pain and pleasure points. You'll create your own original framework that shows exactly how you help your clients go from point A to point B to get the outcome they desire. Clarity also includes mapping out your business model with offers that are desirable for your ideal clients and fulfilling for you to provide. When you put time and energy into actions that give you this kind of clarity about who you serve, what problem you solve, and what you offer, you're focusing on client-getting activities that fall into the category of clarity.

2) ATTRACT

Attract is about magnetizing an audience of followers who resonate deeply with the 3 P language that you use. It's about creating content and experiences that appeal to the people you want to serve. When you regularly take actions to attract an audience of ideal potential clients, you are spending your time on client-getting activities that fall into the category of attract.

3) NURTURE

Nurture is about creating a genuine relationship with the audience of ideal potential clients that you've attracted. They come to know, like, and trust you because of the experiences you create for them when you talk about and display your work. They are hungry to engage with you and work with you because they desire the outcome that you provide and they feel supported by your expertise. When you spend time creating ways for your clients to engage with you by consuming your content, learning from you, or by experiencing your work in some way, you are spending your time on client-getting activities that fall into the category of nurture.

4) INVITE

Invite is about continuously inviting your audience to say yes to engaging with you, whether it's a Free Easy Yes, a low to medium price point yes, or a high price point yes. Making consistent invitations to your audience is what helps them to move along the client pathway that you've designed for them. This helps them go from where they are when they find you, to where they want to be. When you make invitations to your audience that ask them to engage with you, you are spending time on client-getting activities that fall into the category of invite.

5) INSPIRE

Inspire is about welcoming paying clients with heart, excitement, and integrity. It's about learning to become a medium who feels confident and proud to make an offer and to share their skills to help others. Inspire focuses on client-getting activities that turn a potential client into a paying customer like using powerful testimonials, creating thorough and compelling FAQ responses and sales pages, and making it clear how they can expect to benefit from working with you. Any time a follower decides to become a client, many of the client-getting actions you've taken that fall into the category of inspire will be significant.

When your daily, weekly, and monthly actions consistently fall within these five categories, generating consistent revenue and making an impact becomes the natural outcome. We'll be going in depth into each of these categories throughout the rest of this book. By the end, you'll have crafted a day-to-day plan of exactly what to focus on in your business to start making a living as a medium.

CHAPTER 5

CLARITY

UNDERSTANDING YOUR IDEAL CLIENT FOR A PROFITABLE BUSINESS FOUNDATION

You're spending time in the clarity category when you're doing any work in your business that helps you to identify and understand your ideal client. It is any work you put into designing desirable offers for your ideal client, free or paid. It is any work you put into designing a profitable business model. Everything in the clarity category includes work you do in your business to understand *exactly who* you help, *what* problem you help them solve, and *how*.

UNDERSTANDING YOUR IDEAL CLIENT AND GATHERING INFORMATION

It's time to revisit the 3 Ps in order to thoroughly understand who your ideal client is. Perhaps you've already put some work into your 3 Ps for your ideal client. If not, it's time to bring to mind someone you *know* who you feel is your ideal client. When I began my online marketing business I worked with a woman who was my absolute ideal client and everything I wrote or created in my business was designed particularly for Lauren! It helps so much to think of a real person that you know because it's easier to create lists for each of the 3 Ps. Take a moment to bring someone to mind now and answer these questions below.

1. *What are their biggest pain points that you can address? What are they struggling with the most?*
2. *What are their relevant desires? What is the outcome they want most?*
3. *What defines them that makes them an ideal client? What gender are they? What are their belief systems? How old are they?*

Now make a list for each of the 3 Ps for this ideal client. If you'd like, you can give them a new name and make them an avatar based on this person you know. I've shown an example below of my client avatar, Megan.

Person (Megan)	Pain	Pleasure
Woman	Lost her sister	Wants to feel spiritually connected with her sister
Parent/Mother	Aging parents	To feel peace about her parents and for them to be healthy
Kind-hearted	Takes on the emotions of others easily	To have healthier emotional boundaries
Spiritually inclined	Struggles with her connection to Spirit at times	To feel strongly connected to Spirit
Emotionally intelligent	Struggles to separate her emotions from other people's	To be able to more easily separate her emotions from other people's

Therapist	Isn't as accurate as she'd like with mediumship	To be more accurate as a medium
In her 40s	Didn't get to say goodbye to her sister	To know that her sister knows she loves her
Married	Feels guilt because she didn't speak to her sister much before her sister died	To let go of guilt and make peace with the relationship she had with her sister when she was alive
Empathic	Feels that others don't always understand her sensitivity	Accept and take ownership of her sensitivity
Sensitive	Can be a people pleaser to her own detriment	Can do what's right for her guilt free
Humanitarian	Is sensitive to the state of the world	Knows how to care for herself when the world is overwhelming
Has a son and daughter	Struggles with mediumship cycles	Trust Spirit when she goes through different mediumship cycles
Average height, slim, brown hair, brown eyes	Doesn't feel her evidence during a reading is specific enough	To get specific, jaw-dropping evidence when she gives readings

You can have as long a list as you want for each of the Ps. The more detailed you get in terms of knowing and understanding your ideal client and their desires and struggles, the better you'll be at speaking their language and creating offers they really want.

Once you complete your 3 P lists, it's time to make sure you're on the money by going out into the world and talking to people who fit the description of your ideal client!

SURVEYING YOUR CLIENTS

I remember when I ran my group program, *Underearner to Unforgettable* (U2U), I got the idea to create an alumni version as well. After a client would finish the program their first time, they had the opportunity to go through again and continue to reap the benefits of being in my community and scaling their business further.

The first time I offered the alumni round, only three people re-enrolled. I was surprised because I knew there were so many pros to going through the program a second time. About two thirds of the way through the next launch of U2U, I sent out a survey to my clients. I asked them questions like, "What are you enjoying most in the program?" "What do you want more of?" "What do you want less of?" "What suggestions can you make to improve U2U even more?" "Are you thinking about enrolling again as an alumni?" "What bonus(es) could I add that would make it a no-brainer to enroll again for an alumni round?"

When I got the survey results back, the answers were chock full of juicy bonus ideas that students were excited about. One was an alumni-only coaching call. Another was a training call to review their finished websites. The information I garnered from my survey was priceless. I came to know *exactly* what my clients loved best about my program and even more importantly, I understood the things they felt they still needed. It was as simple as using their bonus ideas from the surveys and adding them in when students returned for an alumni round! Many of my students stayed for *more* than two rounds of the program. By the time I decided to retire my online marketing business, I had run eight rounds of U2U. The last seven times that included my survey, 50% or more of my U2Uers re-enrolled in the alumni round.

I've always been a big fan of surveying your clients and conducting market research! It's the thing that helps you create a business that features an offer that your ideal client will actually say yes to. In the conversation that I had with my friend in the coffee shop, not only did she show me an AI bot that could answer customer support questions, she also asked me the most important tasks that I wish AI could do for me in my business. This is an example of her doing her research and "surveying" me. She even said during the conversation that hearing from me in this way helped her design offers that other high performing spiritual entrepreneurs would say yes to.

It's time to create 15 questions for your ideal client to answer during the interviews you'll be conducting. That's right, I want you to go and chat to *at least* ten people who you feel are your ideal client and hear exactly what they have to say about their pain points, pleasure points, and what they think might solve their problems. I suggest you select the top 10 questions you feel will give you the answers you need in order to understand, speak to, and attract your ideal clients.

Coming up with 15 questions to ask your ideal client during an interview is great practice for thinking from the perspective of your ideal client. We want your mind to get used to contemplating the thoughts, needs, pain points, and pleasure points of your ideal client from just about every angle.

As you collect this information, you'll continue to hone your communication skills like how to speak to your ideal clients using their exact words, let them know you understand what they're going through and you're the best person to help them. Think of this as a chance to let your target market write your messaging for you!

The best questions to ask your ideal clients are questions that will give you specific examples of all three of the Ps (pain, pleasure, and person) as well as their interest in any tools or modalities that you use to help your clients get results. Examples of tools might be crystals, tarot cards, tea leaves, or any other "prop" that you use to conduct your spiritual work. Modalities might be mediumship, psychic work, reiki, breathwork, tapping, etc.

Additionally, you can ask them questions about their willingness to invest and at what level or run any details by them about offers you're thinking of putting together. If you don't have any ideas about your offers yet, no worries. We'll get to that next! You can let your interviewees know that you'd love to interview them again once you put together your offer.

Another good rule of thumb is to ask simple, specific questions. For example, you'll get a less specific (and therefore less useful) answer if you were to ask them, "What's your number one desire when it comes to your connection to Spirit? Your mediumship? A development circle?" all at once as one multi-part question, rather than breaking that question into three separate questions:

"What's your number one desire when it comes to your connection to Spirit?"

"What's your number one desire when it comes to your mediumship?"

"What would you want most from a mediumship development circle?"

Open-ended questions are also useful because they ensure that you're not accidentally leading your prospect to an answer. For example, a multiple choice answer gives them only limited options and isn't giving them a blank canvas to voice whatever comes up for them first. Two great examples of open-ended questions are: "What would you like more of?" "What would you like less of?" If you do want to know how genuinely interested they are in something that you'd like to offer, you could give them a detailed description and then ask how interested they are, or how true something is for them, on a scale of 1 - 10 and why. Below are a few of my favorite questions to use when I survey my clients. For each question, I give the formula for the question first and then an example below.

1. What would motivate you to hire someone to help you *(overcome your pain point and achieve your pleasure point)?*

   Ex. What would motivate you to hire someone to help you *(develop your mediumship/reconnect with your passed loved one)?*

2. What's your greatest challenge in relation to *(experiencing your pleasure point)?*

   Ex. What's your greatest challenge in relation to *(developing your mediumship/finding a great medium)?*

3. As a *(describe your P for person)* who wants to *(their pleasure point),* what frustrates you?

   Ex. As a *(person who is grieving the loss of a loved one and who is interested in developing their mediumship),* what frustrates you?

4. As a *(describe your P for person)* who wants to *(their pleasure point),* what do you want more of?

   Ex. As a *(person who is grieving the loss of a loved one and who is interested in developing their mediumship),* what do you want more of?

5. What's the max amount of money you'd spend to have that result? To hire someone to help you with that?

6. What's the ideal amount of time you think you'd need that support in order to reach your result?

Now it's time to put together 15 survey questions of your own and start interviewing your ten ideal clients. Feel free to use your own versions of the examples I've created above for a portion of your questions and remember that the best questions will help you discover specific details about each of your three Ps: the person, their pain points, and their pleasure points! Take lots of notes, stay curious, and make sure you listen carefully to every word they say and *how* they say it. You can tell when someone feels extremely enthusiastic about something vs. when they are only mildly interested.

I've heard clients tell me before that they have a hard time tracking down ten people to survey. If that's the case for you, tap your extended network for their connections. Perhaps you are a member of a spiritual group or a spiritualist church. I promise you, if you ask and ask, you'll easily find ten ideal clients to speak with.

Whether or not you find the task of interviewing fun, you can learn a lot from simply observing your ideal clients. I like to look up experts who are conducting the same work I am and then become a follower to check out what kind of content they are creating. If I were to search on YouTube, I could see the titles of their videos and which videos seem to be getting the most views. I could type into Google a question I think they might ask and see what juicy content comes up that they've created. I could watch them on Instagram or any other social platforms and see what their followers are saying. You can also look online for mediumship or spiritual books that have four and five-star reviews and check out their table of contents and the reviews they've received. You could sign up for a mediumship class if you want to see the questions other mediums ask or the skills they want to learn. You could get a reading from a medium to put yourself in your ideal clients' shoes and experience first hand what they will experience when they sit with you. The ways and places to observe your ideal clients are endless.

An important thing to keep in mind is that this is your market research and will help you better understand your person, as well as their pain and pleasure points. You are not surveying them to rip off other people's content or to plagiarize. While I'm sure this isn't what you have in mind, use this practice *only* to be curious about your ideal client. When we get to the part where we put together your offer(s), focus on generating your own original ideas!

Now that you've surveyed *at least* ten people who fit your ideal client profile, are you surprised at just how much you've learned? If you're anything like me, you've probably had all kinds of ideas about how you can help them. Maybe you've discovered pain and pleasure points that you wouldn't have thought of. You most certainly will have hit the jackpot when it comes to hearing the language they use to talk about their desires and struggles! All of the information that you've gathered is priceless. Knowing your ideal client like the back of your hand is essential to being able to speak their language and create offers that have them saying, "I need that!" Now, I highly recommend reviewing your 3 P lists. Is there anything that you'd like to change on your lists or details that you'd like to add? Are you going to keep the same client avatar that you had been thinking about when you first began, or do you want to slightly tweak something about them now that you have more clarity about who your ideal client really is? Take some time to reflect upon your 3 Ps before moving on. I promise you won't regret it. Many entrepreneurs skip over or rush this part of the process and are sorry later. Your 3 Ps are a vital part of the foundation of your entire business, and if something is off because you don't quite understand the nuances of your P for person, you won't be able to make a living with the offers and business model that you create.

It's time to create your *Who I Work With* 3 P statement! Now that you've interviewed your ideal clients, conducted research, and finalized your 3 P table, it's time to make sure people feel like you're speaking directly to them by crafting an introductory statement. If they're questioning whether or not your offer is meant specifically for them, they may hesitate and pass you by, but by having a clear message upfront, you can persuade them immediately. This statement will be helpful in moments when people ask you what you do and will help you introduce yourself online or in person. Most importantly, once you craft your statement, you can check any marketing you create against it. Ideally, every word you say or experience you create for your followers should align with it. That means you're constantly speaking to that one specific person—your client avatar—and you're showing them in your language not only what you do, but that you're aware of their pain and pleasure points, and you're an expert at helping them find solutions.

Now that you've done the work and filled in the 3 P table, creating your statement should come easily. It'll be like creating a Mad Lib sentence, which happens to be one of my favorite things to do! Below I've created a statement and all you have to do is fill in the person, and the pain and pleasure points. I've given three examples below of different statements that might resonate with you. These are statements that fit well for me, so make sure to create an original one that aligns uniquely to you.

I work with _____ who are struggling with _____
        (person)   (pain point)

and instead want to _____ so that they can _____.
                  (pleasure point)   (pleasure point)

> *Ex #1: I work with aspiring mediums who want a stronger connection to Spirit and to be able to work professionally so they can make a living as a medium.*

> *Ex #2: I work with aspiring mediums who want a stronger connection to Spirit and to be able to work professionally so that they can make a positive difference by helping their clients find peace and healing.*

> *Ex #3: I work with those who have lost a loved one, who are struggling with grief, and who want to find peace so that they can heal and enjoy life again.*

Your turn!

I work with _____ who are struggling with _____
                (person)   (pain point)

and instead want to _____ so that they can _____.
                (pleasure point)   (pleasure point)

CREATING YOUR FRAMEWORK

When it comes to creating a really fantastic offer, and marketing that offer, it's helpful to have a framework that clarifies the overarching system that you use to bring your people from where they are when they come to you, to where they ultimately desire to be after having your support. First, we want to map out how you take your clients from point A to point B. Then we'll use that as a foundation to structure your offers and the journey your clients will take while working with you in that offer.

Even if your clients come to you at different stages, with different skills, or somewhat different needs, your framework should support them regardless of where they are on their journey, ***and*** give you the ability to meet them where they are. For example, even though I considered my U2U program to be absolutely ideal for beginning entrepreneurs, almost 50% of my students had been running their own businesses for 3+ years. While a beginner might need to work hard to lay the groundwork for the clarity part of the Client Attraction Framework, a more advanced student might be looking to create better lead magnets to focus on building a larger audience. That means the more advanced student might spend more time on the attract lever. Regardless of being at different stages, the Client Attraction Framework serves both of them.

The super-duper cool thing about your framework is that it can serve as an outline for a single offer, multiple offers, free downloadable or live content, a course, a part of a book you might write, and so much more. Your framework will also help you gain clarity about the different possibilities for your ultimate business model down the road. You'll see what I mean as we journey through this part of the book.

Before we begin designing your framework, we're going to discuss the two different kinds of frameworks that you might create. If you are going to be teaching your ideal clients *how* to do something, like develop their mediumistic skills, then you'll be creating a Client Results Framework. The Client Results Framework is about helping your ideal client develop skills that will take them from point A to point B so that they can get the result they came to you for.

If you are not interested in teaching your ideal clients anything, but instead you want to provide them with an *experience* that moves them from point A to point B, you'll be creating a Client Experience Framework. For example, let's say that you want to offer private mediumship readings, spiritual assessments, and group readings. In this case, your framework will outline the steps *you* take as you provide your ideal clients with the experience of a reading that will move them from point A to point B.

If you plan to teach your clients to get a certain result, but you also have offers that give them an experience, you might want to create each kind of framework. For example, my development circle and courses teach my clients to get a certain result, like developing their mediumistic skills. This is when I use my Client Results Framework. When I give a reading that enables them to have an experience but isn't teaching them a skill, then I use my Client Experience Framework.

As you break down your process for helping your clients with either of these frameworks, you provide yourself with incredible clarity about *how* you do what you do. This can be helpful in terms of finding compelling ways to differentiate and talk about your work to entice potential clients to become customers. There are many more benefits, like how the details of each of these kinds of frameworks can give you ideas for multiple free and paid offers you might create.

For now, choose whether you'll start by creating a Client Results Framework or a Client Experience Framework. To create your framework, we'll follow a simple step-by-step process so that you feel clear about the support that you provide. From there, you'll construct and price your offer(s). Once you've done that, you can come back and create an additional framework.

I'll show you how to create a framework using my Mediumship Development Framework as an example. Later on in this chapter I'll be sharing an example of my Client Experience Framework as well.

Our first step in creating your framework is to define where your clients tend to be when they come to you (point A) and where they'd ultimately like to get to with your support (point B). I've found with many of my clients that their ideal client is a version of their former self. Perhaps this is true for you and you can remember being at point A and then going on your journey to get to point B. This is one way that some entrepreneurs become experts at helping their ideal clients who are in similar situations. It may be that you haven't experienced your ideal client's A to B journey, but that you've developed specific skills or had training that allows you to under-stand their needs and help them move from point A to point B.

In either case, you need to have the skills to support your clients to make the changes and to get the results that you're telling them are possible. Below I've shared an example of point A and point B for my ideal client that my Client Results Framework is based on.

Ideal Client Journey Point A:
Describe below the state/circumstance that your ideal client tends to be in, or the need(s) that they have when they come to you for support.

My ideal client has usually lost a loved one in the past. They are often just becoming aware of their mediumistic abilities through a single or multiple spiritual awakenings. They are very interested in developing their mediumistic skills and want to be able to provide a full suite of mediumship services and experiences. They don't feel that they have control over their spiritual gifts at all or are not at a level where they'd feel confident calling themselves professionals. They often need practice getting specific evidence, identifying spirits, interpreting spiritual impressions, or working with multiple spirits. They also feel isolated as a spiritual seeker and don't feel they have a place to go for trustworthy information and community.

Ideal Client Journey Point B:
Describe below the state/circumstance that your ideal client desires to be in, or the goal that they'd like to have achieved after they've had your support.

My ideal client desires to feel that the grief from their loss does not overcome their ability to connect to Spirit. They would like to have more perspective about their spiritual awakening(s) and feel that the experience has been normalized. This will allow them to release fear and find comfort and joy with their spiritual gifts and experiences. They have developed their skills to a high level of proficiency in terms of speaking with spirits. They are able to give powerful readings to people, both free and paid, that help their sitters move through their grief, find peace, and receive the healing that mediumship provides. They feel they have more control over their mediumistic gifts and are confident enough to call themselves a medium or even work professionally if that is their desire. They have learned how to get specific evidence, identify spirits, interpret impressions more accurately, and work with multiple spirits. They have found a community of like-minded people who understand and support them as a medium.

Now that you're clear on the point A to point B of your ideal client, it's time to get the juices flowing about *how* you help your clients get results and create transformation for themselves. We'll do this by listing all the ways that you help your clients. We'll call these different ways of helping your clients "tools." Your tools include any topics that you teach, skills, methods, step-by-steps, modalities, etc. that help your client move themselves from point A to point B.

Don't hold back here or worry about listing them in any particular order. Use this exercise to brainstorm *everything* about *how* you help your clients and we'll organize the information into your Client Results Framework afterward. Sharing every little thing you can think of will help you to construct your Client Results Framework more easily.

I've shared below an example of twenty different tools that I use to help my clients transition from aspiring mediums (point A) to highly skilled mediums (point B). These tools make up my Client Results Framework which I call my Mediumship Development Framework. Make the list as long as you possibly can. While my list only includes 20 tools, I have many more.

Tools

Sitting in the power	Meditation	Remote viewing	Using and understanding spiritual files
How to become a clear channel	Exercises to handle hearing "no"	How to increase your confidence as a medium	Automatic writing
How to find/ develop a spiritual community	How to calm your nerves with a physical cue	Exercises to handle tricky sitters	Creating spiritual boundaries
How to work with multiple spirits	Noticing sounds for clairaudience development	How to give a spiritual assessment	How to create symbols with Spirit
How to identify a spirit	Mediumship ethics	The difference between psychic and mediumistic work	How to cycle through the clairs for better evidence

Now that you've got your list of tools which include any topics that you teach, skills, methods, step-by-steps, modalities, etc., it's time to design your Client Results Framework. Think of it as a high-level view, or map, of the systematic journey you support your clients along.

It's empowering to know that you have an original framework of your own that you base your work on, and that your clients can follow. As well as being a confidence booster, it's a game changer when it comes to being able to clearly describe *how* you do what you do. If someone asks, "How do you help your clients?" or "What would working together look like?" you'll have a concise and compelling response that may very well lead to them wanting to know more.

If you're worried that no system exists for the work that you do, I want to let you know that I've never found that to be the case for any client I've worked with. There may not be a system in place yet, but I assure you that no matter what you offer, there is some kind of method to the madness. Even better, it's likely teachable, leverageable, and even delegatable.

Keep in mind that simplicity is key. While I've seen CRFs that are three steps, seven steps, or even nine, I'm a huge fan of making them easily digestible for even the most beginner prospective clients. Having a CRF that is just 5 steps makes it easy for me, and them, to digest powerful content snippets without getting overwhelmed or confused. Remember that the confused or overwhelmed customer often says no.

To begin designing your CRF, think about the steps you've taken, or that you help your clients take, to go from point A to point B. I've left space for 7 steps below, but feel free to use less if you'd like. You may find that some of your topics, methods, or modalities may function better as tools rather than steps of their own. Think of the steps as the overarching path that your client will take without fussing too much about the details that fall under the step.

If you look at the list of my tools below, you'll see that this version has some of the tools of my CRF circled. Each of the boxes that is circled in red felt to me like it was either an actual step itself, or a topic that was under a step that felt obvious for me. For example, "noticing sounds for clairaudience development" is a topic under the step, *Communication and the Clairs.* The three squares that are circled in green are three topics that fit under my fifth step, *Command of Craft.* Listing these twenty different tools, or ways, that I help my clients advance their mediumship helped me start to see how many overarching steps I needed in my Client Results Framework.

Tools

Sitting in the power	Meditation	Remote viewing	Using and understanding spiritual files
How to become a clear channel	Exercises to handle hearing "no"	How to increase your confidence as a medium	Automatic writing
How to find/ develop a spiritual community	How to calm your nerves with a physical cue	Exercises to handle tricky sitters	Creating spiritual boundaries
How to work with multiple spirits	Noticing sounds for clairaudience development	How to give a spiritual assessment	How to create symbols with Spirit
How to identify a spirit	Mediumship ethics	The difference between psychic and mediumistic work	How to cycle through the clairs for better evidence

What I've shared below are the five overarching steps that make up my Client Results Framework that I've titled my *Mediumship Development Framework.* The overarching steps that you use to help your clients move from point A to point B will perfectly describe *how* you help your clients get results.

Step 1	Step 2	Step 3	Step 4	Step 5
Clear Channel	Communication and the Clairs	Confidence	Community	Command of Craft

Now it's your turn to decide upon the steps that'll make up your framework. If one of your tools feels like an overarching part of *how* you move your client from point A to point B, that could be a sign that it's one of your main steps. Don't worry about the tools that you're leaving out from your steps right now. In the next part of this process, you'll see how to add them back in.

Once you've decided upon the overarching steps you'll help your client take for your Client Results Framework, add the tools under each step so that you and your clients understand *how* you help them take each step. Check out the example of my Client Results Framework with the remaining 20 tools added back in, plus a few extras.

Step 1	Step 2	Step 3	Step 4	Step 5
Clear Channel	*Communication and the Clairs*	*Confidence*	*Community*	*Command of Craft*
Sitting in the power	Remote viewing (Clairvoyance)	Exercises to handle hearing "no"	How to find/develop a spiritual community	Using and understanding spiritual files
Meditation	Automatic writing (Claircognizance)	How to increase your confidence as a medium	How to find a good mediumship mentor	Creating spiritual boundaries
Decluttering	Noticing sounds (Clairaudience)	How to calm your nerves with a physical cue	How to find a good development circle	How to work with multiple spirits
Taking care of your physical health	How to identify a spirit (multiple clairs)	Exercises to handle tricky sitters		How to give a spiritual assessment
	Cycling the clairs (multiple clairs)			Creating symbols with Spirit
				Mediumship ethics
				The difference between psychic and mediumistic work

While I have many more tools that fall under each of my five steps, the ones that I've shared give you an idea of how to organize your CRF.

Can you see how any one of these boxes could be a content topic for you on social media, in an email to your list, a free download to have your followers become subscribers, or perhaps a course, class, or training workshop? What's even better is that once you create powerful content on any one of these topics or steps, you can repurpose it. Maybe you make a short video on social media and then you transcribe it to use as an email for your list.

When someone asks me what I do, I can say that I'm a medium and I also teach mediumship. If someone were to ask me, "How do you teach mediumship?" I'd answer by saying, "I focus on the five most important aspects of mediumship to help my clients become better mediums." They might ask me then, "What are the five most important aspects?"

I'd reply, "Becoming a clear channel, spirit communication and the clairs, confidence, creating a community of mediums, and developing a command of their craft." As they become more curious they might say, "How do you teach your clients confidence?" I would then answer by saying, "One of my favorite ways to do this is giving my students exercises to practice hearing 'no' from a sitter. Sometimes I'll have them conduct a practice reading with another student in class. No matter what they bring through from a spirit, I'll instruct their partner to say 'no.' This helps them get used to 'nos' and avoid dropping their confidence, and vibration, when it happens."

If you're wanting to create a Client Experience Framework, remember that the difference between a Client Results Framework and a Client Experience Framework is that the CEF is about the steps *you* take to help your client have a certain experience that moves them from point A to point B. I'd love to begin by sharing with you my list of 20 tools that I use to help my clients move from point A to point B when I give them a reading.

Warmly welcome them	Explain how mediumship works	Explain how I work as a medium	Get consent to give them a reading
Say my intention/ prayer	Ask how they found out about me	Send them a confirmation email and reminders	Send them an educational prep video
Blend w/ a spirit, their aura, or a guide	Bring through evidence that can be validated	Avoid asking questions	Ask permission if sensitive information comes up
Present a body of information and check for validation	Stay aware of my sitter and create a rapport with them	Close the reading so they know it's over	Allow them to share context and feedback after the reading
Follow up with them for feedback	Ask if I have permission to use their reading online	Ask if I can use their feedback as a testimonial on my website and in my marketing materials	Tell them I appreciate any referrals and recommendations

Now that I've created a list of 20 ways that I can move my client from point A to point B, I can look through all of these tools and see what steps seem to make the most sense. If you're creating a Client Experience Framework, you may find that 20 tools isn't enough. Make your list as long as you possibly can to help illuminate what your overarching steps might be. Even if you ultimately decide that you won't include some of the tools you list as a step or a tool underneath a step, everything that you list can still be helpful for outlining your overarching system.

Once you've created your long list of tools, it's time to create the steps for your Client Experience Framework. Below I've shared an example of mine called the *Sitter Experience Framework*.

Step 1	Step 2	Step 3	Step 4	Step 5
Preparation	*Permission*	*Profession*	*Presentation*	*Perception*

I'm most definitely one for alliteration. You can see that each step starts with a P in this framework, whereas my CRF features the 5 Cs! I discovered these steps by studying all of the different tools that I use to move my client from point A to point B. As I read through each of the tools, I noticed that groups of them fit under different umbrellas. Below I've shared how I categorized each of my tools under the steps that I shared with you above. You might also notice that I added in topics as I finalized my CEF. Once you understand the overarching steps, it becomes even easier to understand all of the different tools or topics that you can list underneath them.

Step 1	Step 2	Step 3	Step 4	Step 5
Preparation	*Permission*	*Profession*	*Presentation*	*Perception*
Agreement, confirmation and reminders	Get consent	Blend w/ a spirit, their aura, a guide, etc.	Efficient and effective use of language	Allow them to share context and feedback
Prep video	Make sure they're comfortable	(mediumship) Identify the spirit(s)	Present a body of information (about five pieces of evidence) and check for validation	Day after thanks and follow up
Welcome	Intention/Prayer	(mediumship) Bring through evidential communication from the spirit(s)	Trust Spirit by speaking with confidence	Permission to use the reading
How mediumship works		(mediumship) Deliver a meaningful message	Ask permission if sensitive information comes up	Testimonial inquiry
How I work as a medium		(mediumship) Close: leave the sitter with the spirit's love	Avoid asking direct questions	Referrals and recommendations
			Manage the reading when obstacles arise	
				The difference between psychic and mediumistic work

If I want to attract clients who want a reading, I can create content about any one of these steps or tools to showcase my skill, knowledge, and professionalism. For example, I might create content about *the top five things to look for to make sure you're with a credible medium* and discuss any of the tools from steps two through four. This kind of content, paired with recordings of my readings can very effectively position me as a credible expert and attract clients who resonate with my style of working.

Once you've completed your framework(s), give yourself a huge congrats. This is a foundational piece of your business. Don't worry if you're not sure whether it's perfect yet. It's a mapped out system that you can continue to adjust and to use with your clients to help them get results. Before we jump into designing your offers, I'd like to share some additional things to think about in terms of your framework.

1. It's not always necessary that every tool is utilized with every client. Meet your clients where they are. It's usually best to give them only what they need to help them focus.
2. If someone asks me how I work with my clients, I don't begin by going into the details that fall under each and every step. I focus on succinctly sharing my overarching steps so that my explanation is clear and quick. If you do this well, it's possible that they'll be ready to hear more!
3. Remember that your framework will help you in many ways beyond just designing your offers. You can use it as a way to decide what topics you could create content about online, for a training or workshop, or even in a book. As one of your "for the future" offers, you could make a course out of just one of your steps, or many of them.
4. Having this map that outlines your system and all of the tools you use can also help you more easily identify an area

of your work that you might specialize in, or love best, from your process. For example, I created a training that focused solely on what I do before and after my readings to make sure they go smoothly with little to no client drama.

5. Worry less about getting this perfect and focus more on putting together your first rendition of a system that you have confidence in and can refine over time. Just knowing your framework will help you feel clear, prepared, and able to recognize the value you have to offer!

CREATING AND PRICING YOUR OFFER(S)

Let's review what kind of offers you might create.

When Just Starting:

- One offer that helps you stay relevant, sharpen your craft and expertise, and is low-cost in terms of resources required.
- One offer that can become a cash cow, help you leverage your business, and is low-cost in terms of resources required.

For the Future (Once Your Initial Offers Are Validated):

- One offer that has the potential to be a *major* cash cow, create massive leverage, and is low to high-cost in terms of resources required.
- One offer that has the potential to create more passive income, and is low to high-cost in terms of resources required. *(Optional)*

For my offer that helps me stay relevant, sharpen my craft and expertise, and is low-cost in terms of resources required, I chose a mediumship reading. Because my main focus is mediumship *and* I specialize in bringing through messages from passed human loved ones from the other side, this fits perfectly for me. Let's say that I was primarily an animal communicator who worked with both living and passed animals. In that case, my first offer might be psychic animal readings with a living animal or mediumistic readings with a passed animal, or both.

Giving readings consistently, even if it's not a large number of readings, helps me to continue to feel confident in my work. For a long time, my price for readings was $250. I gave an average of about nine readings a month. That allowed me to create $27,000 a year from one-on-one readings. This revenue alone is not something I could live off of, which is why it's so important that you think about a second offer that can help you leverage. Before we get there, think about what your offer might be to help you stay relevant, sharpen your craft and expertise, and is low-cost in terms of resources required.

Once you've made that decision, decide on an additional offer that has the potential to become a cash cow, to help you leverage, and that is relatively low-cost in terms of resources required. We're looking for an offer that is not trading dollars for hours by working one-on-one. Instead, we want an offer that can multiply our impact and income by serving many at once. The other important detail is that this offer shouldn't be a high-cost offer in terms of resources required. Remember the example I shared in both chapter three and chapter four about how creating a course is very high-cost in terms of the resources of time, money, and energy that is required? We want to choose something that takes a lot less cost output. I chose to create a mediumship development circle for this second offer, because it fits all of the criteria that I've listed. In my first full year of offering three mediumship development circles with 14 students each, I was able to create about $20,000 in revenue each quarter of the year. The two offers combined create $107,000 a year. Can you see why it was so important to have my second offer?

While I could have tried to give more and more readings, that would have been much more tiring for me, and most definitely not sustainable. I would have to give four times the amount of readings to hit the same revenue. While it would be the same amount of time spent, I'd be helping far fewer people, and I'd be using a lot more energy while being less fulfilled emotionally and creatively. I love teaching and I know that for my business model to be sustainable in all ways, I have to be able to serve multiple people at a time and diversify the ways in which I help my clients. What might your offer be that can become a cash cow, help you leverage, and is low-cost in terms of resources required?

For both of these offers, I feel incredibly confident about how I'll be helping my clients move from point A to point B. This is because of the frameworks that I've outlined for both of them. For my first offer, my mediumship reading, I know that I'll be using the *Sitter Experience Framework* 5 Ps— preparation, permission, profession, and presentation to create a memorable experience of healing and connection. For my second offer, my mediumship development circle, I know that I'll be using my *Mediumship Development Framework* that focuses on the 5 Cs. These five Cs are the most important aspects of mediumship that will help my clients move from aspiring mediums to highly proficient mediums. I can point to any tool or step in my Client Results Framework to design the exercises that I'll be taking my clients through in their weekly sessions. I can switch things up and keep them interesting for me and my clients by choosing tools and steps that fit with the needs of my different students in each of my circles.

When it comes to pricing your offer, there are three things that I take into consideration:

1. **What do I believe is the value or worth of my offer?**
   What kind of outcomes do I feel are possible for my client when they invest in this experience for themselves? Benefits might include: releasing stress and grief, feeling more connected to deceased loved ones, experiencing greater well-being, and improving relationships with both the living and the departed.

2. **What's the industry standard for other offers that may be similar to mine?** What do I think my clients are willing to invest? It's a great idea to research other mediums or spiritual practitioners that you respect and see what price points their one-on-one readings or spiritual sessions are at.

3. **What price feels best to me that excites me and feels like I'm stretching, but also still allows me to feel confident in my ability to hear yes?** I side on choosing a price that feels relatively easy for you to receive but good in terms of being fair compensation, to begin. The cool thing about being your own boss is that you can shift your prices when you want or need to. What I *do not* suggest doing is setting a price that makes you feel like shitting your pants because it's too much of a stretch. This is a great way to kill your momentum. When you choose a price that feels right after thinking through these criteria, you'll be less inclined to discount your offer due to external pressures.

There's nothing wrong with pro bono clients or offering special pricing. It's a great thing to do as long as you can fit it into your business model in a way that is sustainable for you.

With that in mind, I'd like to share a few cautionary thoughts to be aware of in the instance of discounting when it *doesn't* feel right to you. Perhaps you feel like you're being pressured, or just caving in due to a lack of confidence. Let's talk about the detriment of discounting when it doesn't feel right.

- The client may (and usually sub-consciously does) see your work as less valuable.
- You may feel resentful for getting paid less down the road, or immediately.
- It can weaken your ability to leverage your business and/ or create resources that enable you to spend your time and money on exactly what gives you the most joy and impact.

Conversely, here's what's great about trusting your price.

- If you priced your offer consciously and you've done your research, there are likely people out there who want it and are willing to invest in it.
- You feel great about the energetic exchange that takes place and happy about working with your new client.
- The client is more committed to your work together. This may lead to them being prompt, present, and more likely to do the work required.

With all of this in mind, I do a little goldilocks type of game when I put a price on my offers. I did it for my mediumship readings and I did it for my development circle. I ask myself first, "What price feels too low and like not enough for the energy and effort I expend?" Then I ask myself, "What price feels like too much of a stretch?" Now that I have a range, I ask myself, "What price point feels just right?" Your just right price may feel like a little bit of a stretch, and if you're charging for the first time, it may also make you nervous. That's normal and ok.

Now that you've established the price points for your new offer(s), let's discuss the topic of pay in full pricing and payment plans. I don't tend to offer payment plans for my one-on-one readings. I have my clients pay in full before their reading. This keeps the energetic exchange clean and simple.

Having a payment plan is usually a good option when you have an offer that extends past a single session. My development circle is a good example of this. My clients can pay in full for $555, or they can opt for a payment plan that is three monthly payments of $216, totaling $648. Keeping your payment plan simple is extremely important. Remember that the confused or overwhelmed customer usually says no. If your potential clients ask you what the payment plan is, make it simple and easy to understand. You'll notice that the payment plan often adds up to more than the pay-in-full price. This is to make up for the risk that you take on by receiving payments over time versus immediately. Depending on the industry, many entrepreneurs or business owners who receive recurring payments via debit or credit cards can lose anywhere from 10% - 35% or more of their accounts receivable revenue. In my experience, I lose 5% or less due to the size of my business, the clients I attract, and the way I frontload my expectations with my clients.

I strongly suggest validating these first two offers before you go adding more. Every offer requires time, money, and energy to market. As soon as you can prove that your first two offers are something that your ideal clients are willing to say yes to consistently, you'll start to generate revenue. Once you have cash coming in the door *and* you're profitable, it's a much better time to expand into the "for the future" offers. That being said, depending on your aspirations for your mediumship business, you might decide that you like the simplicity of two offers. For the first 18 months that I was in business, I absolutely loved giving nine readings a month and running three development circles each week for 12 weeks at a time. I took a week off every month from giving readings and between circle sessions, I usually had a week off as well.

If you see yourself creating more offers in the future, and you're close to having your first two offers validated, it's time to think about "for the future" offers.

For the Future (Once Your Initial Offers are Validated):

- One offer that has the potential to be a *major* cash cow, create massive leverage, and is low to high-cost in terms of resources required.
- One offer that has the potential to create more passive income, and is low to high-cost in terms of resources required. *(Optional)*

At one point I realized that if I only wanted 14-16 students tops in each of my development circles, and I was only going to give three readings a week, that I would need to create another highly leveraged offer to be able to significantly multiply my income beyond six figures. While I've heard of development circles that enroll larger numbers of students, I love the intimacy of my circles for now. As I was thinking about my "for the future offer" that has the potential to be a *major* cash cow, create massive leverage, and is low to high-cost in terms of resources required, I decided to create my mediumship course, *Speaking With Spirits*. I've successfully run courses in the past. I know the time, money, and energy they take to create. At the time I first got the idea for this course, I was running a 6-figure business with 60%+ profitability and I knew it was the right time. I also know the revenue that courses have the potential to generate. My *Speaking With Spirits* course can enroll many more students than a development circle and is at a higher price point of $997. I beautifully organized my body of work around mediumship development and created training videos, powerful exercises, and an online forum where students can build relationships and develop community.

Do you have any ideas about what your offer might be, even in the future, that has the potential to be a major cash cow and allow you to leverage your impact and revenue? You don't have to know right at this moment if you're not at that point, but I love to share my example so that you get the wheels turning if you see yourself heading down this path.

Perhaps you're wondering about the second "for the future" offer that I've shared. This is an offer that has the potential to create more passive income, and is low to high-cost in terms of resources required. My example of this "for the future" offer is my YouTube channel. It began as a Free Easy Yes offer that was high-cost due to the large amount of time and energy that it took me to learn how to run my YouTube channel and to create and edit how-to video content and my readings. I did my research and knew that for people like me, who are prolific when it comes to content generation, that YouTube is highly effective in terms of building trust quickly with followers and turning them into paying customers. I also knew that at some point, even if it was a long slow burn, I could monetize my channel and get paid for the ads that would run before and after, and sometimes during, my videos.

There are very few offers that are truly passive in terms of creating income. At some point, most require time, money, and energy. This is why I list this type of offer as optional. It may not be necessary for you. For me, I like to create different offers that generate revenue so that I'm not only relying on one. Most of all, because I enjoy being on video and creating content, I love the idea of my hard work continuing to pay off via revenue from ads, but also the sales I make from my YouTube followers who decide to become clients.

Are you interested in having a "for the future" offer that has the potential to create more passive income, and is low to high-cost in terms of resources required? If so, take some time to brainstorm a few thoughts and even if the time to move on this offer isn't now, perhaps there will come a time in the future once you've validated two or three solid offers that have created a pathway to profitability for you.

I'm sure there are questions coming up for you about where these clients might come from or how you'll be able to move them along your client pathway. In the following chapter, we'll be discussing how to attract your ideal client. In chapter eight, we'll focus on inviting your client to say yes to both free and paid offers. For now, I'm going to show you where I place my "just starting" and "for the future" offers on my Client Pathway Pyramid.

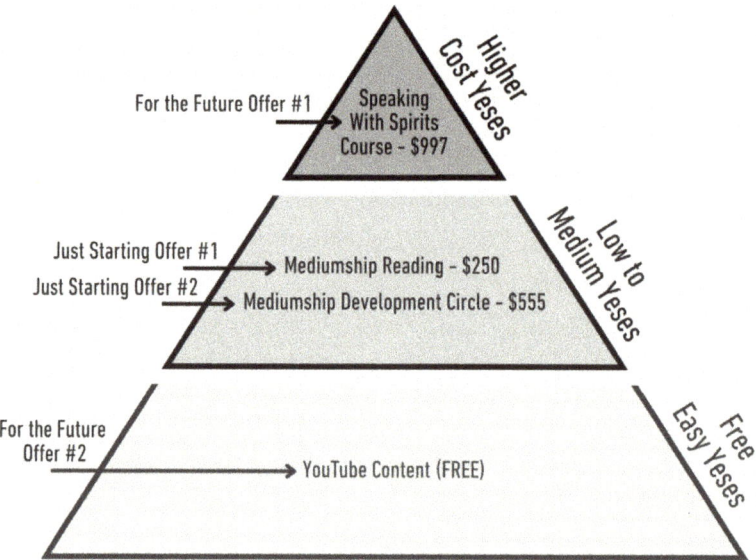

CLIENT PATHWAY PYRAMID
(WITH OFFERS)

For the Future Offer #1 → Speaking With Spirits Course - $997

Higher Cost Yeses

Just Starting Offer #1 → Mediumship Reading - $250
Just Starting Offer #2 → Mediumship Development Circle - $555

Low to Medium Yeses

For the Future Offer #2 → YouTube Content (FREE)

Free Easy Yeses

At this point, one of the most important things is that you understand exactly who your ideal client is. Remember to focus on just one person who you actually know, who perfectly fits as an ideal client. Think about all of the details about them that you're aware of. Speak to them always about their pain points and pleasure points.

It's also crucial that you've made a decision about your "just starting" offers that you know this one specific person would love. It's time to price them and put them on your Client Pathway Pyramid. You can always make changes, but it's important to also make some foundational decisions that you can build upon in the following chapters.

CHAPTER 6

ATTRACT

GROWING YOUR SPIRITUAL COMMUNITY

You're spending time in the attract category when you're doing any work in your business that helps you to attract ideal clients who are hungry to work with you and who feel supported by your expertise. Anything you do that helps you add one more person to your list or as a follower on social media, or who becomes interested from an in-person or online conversation is considered a client-getting action that helps you to attract the right people.

SPEAKING THE LANGUAGE OF YOUR IDEAL CLIENT

Here's the deal. If you want my attention, you've got to say something, or show me something compelling enough to earn it. This is why we went balls to the wall to nail down the 3 Ps of your ideal client. As of 2025, humans are making a decision about whether they're interested in reading your email, purchasing your book, or stopping their scroll on social media in just 2.9 seconds! That's not a lot of time, clearly. If you're going to succeed at attracting a following, you've got to be able to use your words in a super compelling way that shows the value of what you do, and immediately.

Language is powerful and you're not alone if you find it challenging to communicate about your work in a way that is interesting to your people. Your message takes time to develop. It's not an overnight thing. You'll find that just as you will continue to develop and evolve as an individual and a medium, so too will the way you speak in order to attract an audience.

Feeling masterful at talking about what you do requires an ability to tell stories with substance, and use 3 P language. What are stories with substance? Have you ever read an online post or watched a video that got you all fired up? Perhaps it went straight to your heart and truly moved you. Maybe it stopped you in your tracks and made you think. An experience like this occurs when the message is fueled by a powerful story, or a story snippet—a super short story—that connects or conflicts with someone's ultimate values and beliefs. Beneath the words are a strong indication of beliefs and values that attract our ideal clients and repel those who won't be as good of a fit. When we come across a *story with substance* within a marketing message, it creates emotions within us or inspires us to act in some way. Not only that, but the message is memorable—it stands out! Client communication that includes compelling and resonant stories is one of the most powerful ways to attract an audience by *showing* them who you are and what you stand for, instead of literally spelling it out and trying to convince.

In addition to creating content, messaging, and client communication with stories that have substance, we also must become masterful at using 3 P language. Our messaging needs to be able to quickly convey to our audience what's in it for them. Powerful words and moving stories are all around us, but as business owners, we must also include language that clearly illustrates the problem we're here to help solve, and the result we're looking to help our clients create. While I think of the story element as the inspiring energy within a marketing message, I think of the words we use to communicate our value as the 3 P language that structures our messaging. In the first part of this chapter you'll discover how combining these two elements creates compelling communication that attracts ideal clients.

"So what's a *story with substance* again, Mel?" It's any powerful story element within your messaging that communicates your values, beliefs, mission, and/or your deep down why behind what you do. It also resonates deeply with your ideal audience.

Sometimes the wording of an offer can sound sexy and be masterfully focused on the pain points that will be overcome and the results that are possible, but you're just not convinced. In other words, you might see someone market their business with great copy, but it just doesn't feel compelling enough. What's ultimately missing? Story. How thrilling it is when you find someone who you think has the skills and expertise to help you by offering their services, *and* they also have a powerful mission that inspires and motivates you. Perhaps the way their mission, values, beliefs, etc. are represented when they use stories to speak about what they do—even if what they offer is similar to other offers you've seen before—really stands out and makes them unique.

I like to think of injecting stories with substance into my messaging. If I were to write a social media post, inserting even a story snippet here and there can add that extra star quality that gives my messaging a pop. It also makes what I share more memorable.

For example, here's a solid marketing blurb that makes an invitation about joining my development circle, but it's missing the story substance and feels a little soulless to me.

> *Feeling frustrated because you've had too many readings in a row that haven't worked out?*

Wondering how long it will take to be able to consistently give highly accurate readings?

I started focusing on 5 specific aspects of mediumship week in and week out and noticed that I was starting to get rave reviews after my readings!

Join me for my free, live training today and I'll share with you:

- 3 things most mediums don't address when it comes to becoming a clear channel for Spirit with less bias and inaccuracies
- The unique way that I help my clients expand their abilities to use *all* of the clairs (most mentors don't do this with their students!)
- One super important aspect of mediumship that I *never* hear other mentors address that goes *such* a long way to advance your skills
- Three awesome exercises that I use to help my students gain more confidence as mediums so they can bring through jaw-dropping evidence
- *A strategic way* of developing yourself as a medium that can help you finally bring through the evidence that you usually can't get

Here's what it looks like now that I've added in messaging substance.

I saw her looking entirely overcome by her nerves. She was taking shaky shallow breaths to desperately try and calm herself before it was her turn to read. I told her, "Just give what you get and don't worry if it's right or wrong. Trust."

I gave the assignment to hear a song that was meaning-ful to their sitter's passed loved one. My student trusted the spirit she was with and said, "You've got a friend, James Taylor." Her sitter burst into tears, knowing that her loved one was near.

More than 95% of the mediums I work with in my devel-opment circle are afraid of hearing "no." 100% of them want to do the best job they possibly can so they don't let their sitter down.

Wouldn't it be great if you could give a reading with-out being overcome by your fear of getting it wrong? If you're wondering the best way to get there, join me for my live training where I'll be sharing:

- *3 things most mediums don't address when it comes to becoming a clear channel for Spirit with less bias and inaccuracies*
- *The unique way that I help my clients expand their abilities to use* all *of the clairs (most men-tors don't do this with their students!)*
- *One super important aspect of mediumship that I* never *hear other mentors address that goes* such *a long way to advance your skills*
- *Three awesome exercises that I use to help my students gain more confidence as mediums so they can bring through jaw-dropping evidence*
- *A strategic way of developing yourself as a medium that can help you finally bring through the evidence that you usually can't get*

Can you tell the difference between the two? Did you notice that both posts spoke to the benefits that you'll get when you work with me to advance your skills as a medium, but the second had a much more compelling story with substance to it? Did you also notice that without even talking about myself as a mentor, that I was able to convey who I am and how I am to work with, as well as my dedication and belief in my students and the practice of mediumship?

Discovering Yourself Through Story

We'll get to the part where you start crafting your own messaging with plenty of stories that have substance. First, one of my favorite ways to help you begin is by recalling stories from your life that illuminate who you are and what your *mission, values, and beliefs are.* It's one of the first steps to realize things that are unique about you, what's important to you, and why you're doing this work. This is where we begin to start crafting a message that is utterly *you.*

Before I did this exercise, it was difficult to understand what was unique about me. There are plenty of mediums, psychics, and spiritual practitioners to learn from. As I recalled my stories, I began to ask questions about why these were my stories and what about my beliefs and values lead me to these experiences and behaviors. These realizations began to birth and strengthen my motivations behind my work that I was barely conscious of before and unable to articulate.

Through my stories, I noticed my tendency to be deeply passionate, and a visionary with a love for the spiritual aspect of life at the same time that I am very down to earth, analytical, and straightforward. It started to make sense to me why I love evidential mediumship. I like to have proof of the miraculous side of life that we can't always see or measure. I also have iron determination and I will strategically figure out a way to reach just about any goal I set for myself. I enjoy breaking things down step-by-step, but I also use visualization to allow the unseen parts of the universe help me co-create an outcome I desire. This mix of left and right brain, of feminine and masculine, of spiritual and physical is the very essence of me and took me a while to discover. Now, my clients tell me that it's something they appreciate about me and that it's a huge part of why they choose to work with me. Your clients will say the same thing about you as you discover more about yourself and the true and heartfelt motivations behind why you do your work.

I'll share the following stories from my marketing days that still define my approach as a medium, mentor, and leader.

Story #1: Anything Is Possible

When I was 7 or 8 years old, I heard our priest give a homily about how anything is possible with God. I became elated during church! When we got home, I ran straight to my room and changed out of my church dress into my play clothes. I was enlightened. I had realized at that moment that what he was saying was the *truth*! What I had been dreaming of more than anything was how much I desired to fly. We lived out in the country in Idaho. There was a large hill right outside our basement door near the house. I got the biggest running start I possibly could. For a moment, I was sure I *was* flying. Shortly after, I landed on the slope of the hill, and rolled to the bottom, into the bushes and shrubs. I was bruised, yes, but my ego suffered quite a bit more.

- **Values:** humor, adventure, faith, vulnerability, taking risks, joy, enthusiasm, determination, fun, love, magic, miracles, getting out of your comfort zone, belief, spirituality, growth.
- **Beliefs:** If I value humor, determination, taking risks, perhaps a belief is:

I believe in living outside of our comfort zones to expand and grow, and being able to laugh at ourselves when we fail.

- **Skills/Gifts:** Being able to hold the vision for myself and others of what's possible. Unwavering determination and an ability to cultivate a powerful and resilient mentality that leads to never giving up. Being willing to get outside of my comfort zone and risk failure continuously. I'm able to mentor others and help them create confidence in themselves, inspire them, and use humor while doing it. I'm great at holding my clients accountable in a firm but loving way and creating step-by-step tools to help them develop their own high-performance mindset.

Story #2: College Drama

In college, I studied acting and musical theatre. During one of my acting classes, we were assigned scene partners. The goal of the exercise was for each of us to come to the scene with a problem that we had to find a way to solve with the other person's help. The stakes had to be high! We had to stop at nothing to solve each of our own problems with the help of our scene partner, even though they had their own high stakes conflict that they needed our help with.

My emergency was that a friend had gotten in a car accident and I was begging my scene partner to leave the room with me to find help. My scene partner had a friend's blouse that she'd stained, that she absolutely had to get the stain out of before her friend returned. I couldn't convince my scene partner to leave by begging her verbally, so I wrestled the blouse from her. She chased me around the room, trying to get it back, until I turned and threatened that I'd rip the blouse if she didn't come with me. She refused, so I ripped it to shreds, at which point, the class gasped and my scene partner agreed to come with me which ended the scene.

- **Values:** intensity, growth, influence, passion, creativity, adaptability, success, developing skills, presence, determination, innovation, communication, being direct, problem solving, simplification, resilience, persistence.
- **Beliefs:** If I value passion, persistence, and problem solving perhaps a belief is:
  - *I have the skills to help others discover what they are most passionate about and to problem solve endlessly until we find a solution.*
- **Skills/Gifts:** I'm great at strategy, simplifying action steps, and finding that one detail that will change the game instantly. I will stop at nothing. I do whatever it takes… within reason. I'm not afraid to tell it like it is. I don't need people to like me as much as I want them to succeed, and to believe in and respect themselves.

Story #3: Personal Training in Boston

When I lived in Boston, I was a personal trainer at a club. Many of the trainers who were hired got fired, quit, or didn't make enough money because of their failure to build their clientele. I was nervous that I would suffer the same fate. There was a trainer at the club who had created a successful client roster. I began eavesdropping on him during his sales conversations. He would sit in a cubicle with his potential client, and I would sit on the other side of the cubicle and listen to how he conducted the conversation.

When I had my first consultation, I ended the session in the same cubicle as the trainer whom I'd been studying. I conducted the conversation exactly as I'd heard and sold one of the largest packages that the club offered. After my client had paid and we'd scheduled his 1st session, I got a tap on the shoulder. It was the trainer I'd been spying on. He was someone we all looked up to, but he didn't talk much or offer much help to the new recruits. He told me he'd been listening in and offered to mentor me.

- **Values**: curiosity, determination, growth, education, financial empowerment, women making money doing what they love, entrepreneurship, confidence, mastery of craft, leadership, quality, discipline, consistency, communication, sales and making offers, productivity, health, relationships, abundance.
- **Beliefs:** If I value entrepreneurship and financial empowerment perhaps a belief is:
  - *I believe in creating a life where we are fulfilled and paid to share our gifts and make an impact. I believe that all people on this planet should have the opportunity to create resources for themselves doing work that they love.*
- **Skills/Gifts:** I'm a clear communicator. I'm able to inspire and influence others in a positive way, while being firm but loving. I'm a master at the sales conversation and being able to use my words to show the value of my offer. I'm committed to honing my craft. I'm consistent and persistent when it comes to making offers. I can confidently ask for what I want and manage expectations. I have strong boundaries and am unwilling to please others by making false promises or overextending myself.

It's time for you to try out this exercise! To begin, spend a few minutes quieting your mind. With a notebook beside you, be patient as you sit quietly and allow yourself a little walk down memory lane. Write down any stories from your life that come to you. Don't worry about whether the stories are the right ones. It doesn't matter if it's directly related to your work or not. Every story about you is valuable and an extension of who you've become. Now finalize your list with three to five stories.

Here's the fun part, it's story-telling time! Reach out to someone who you like and trust and who will listen objectively. It helps us to relive it with more clarity than if we were to ponder it in our minds on our own. I would suggest keeping your stories short—about five minutes each. I also suggest recording yourself telling the story and listening back afterward. When you do, listen for clues about your values, your beliefs, your natural skills, gifts, and style. After sharing the stories, I listed values, beliefs, and skills that helped me write belief statements and understand more about how I might share these aspects of myself through my messaging.

Using 3 P Language + Tools (Mad Lib Style!)

Now that you understand what stories with substance are and you've been gaining clarity about your values, beliefs, skills, and style, it's time to focus on the second aspect of speaking the language of your ideal client: learning to use 3 P language + tools that shows the humans you're meant to help what's in it for them. The way you compel your audience to see you as an expert and start thinking about working with you comes down to speaking directly to their deepest desires and most craved results, as well as their biggest struggles and pain points. You'll be including words that identify their pain points and illustrate how you can help them reach their desired outcome each and every time that you connect with your audience.

You can also share the tools you use with your clients. For example, here are some tools that work as steps underneath my overarching framework: structuring a mediumistic reading, learning to manage multiple spirits at once, getting better at handling "nos." Other tools that spiritual practitioners use include: tarot cards, tea leaves, and crystals. There are other tools that we might consider modalities like different kinds of energy work, reiki, evidential mediumship, trance mediumship, tapping, and breathwork.

I like to focus on these 3 Ps and tools because it's effective, and it keeps the way we think about communicating with our people simple. Humans invest in themselves for two reasons: to avoid pain and to experience pleasure. Likely, you bought this book because you believe that what you desire is available to you by reading it.

Regardless of what offer you put forth, your ideal client needs to know clearly and quickly that you have the expertise to help them overcome their struggles and realize their desires. Speaking directly to your ideal clients (P for person), letting them know you relate to their struggles (P for pain), and showing them that you've become an expert (who uses certain effective tools) at creating the outcomes and results that they desire (P for pleasure) ultimately communicates to them why investing in themselves and working with you is a no-brainer.

It's important to note that when you include the 3 Ps + tools in your messaging, specificity is key. General pain points ("feeling stuck") and pleasure points ("feeling confident") won't do the trick. You'll see as we continue to master your client communication that the more detailed you are, the more effectively you'll attract the right people. Additionally, you *can* share information about your tools when you speak to your audience. Remember that your tools describe *how* you help your clients overcome pain and experience pleasure. A tool might be a modality that you teach, or a system that you use to bring your clients from point A to point B. When you created your framework, it likely became clear that you have many tools. When it feels right to mention them in your marketing, make sure they are surrounded by the 3 Ps. Why? Ultimately your clients care less about *how* you do what you do, and more about whether or not you can help them overcome their pain and experience their pleasures. It's super common for entrepreneurs to struggle with their brand message, because they act a fool, being a tool, gettin' stuck in what I call Tool Town. Yup, that's when all you do is talk about *how* you do what you do. For example, imagine that someone asks you, "What do you do?" The fatal mistake is turning your tool list into a novel. *"Well, I work with clients to help them when they're energetically stuck because after my kundalini awakening I realized that I'm here to help resolve unwanted forces in the energetic field of our planet, one person at a time. I help them shift their energy and then I help them release stuck energy and then I help them do an energetic protection ceremony and then I..."* It's a sad but sure way to end up clientless. After all, who's going to invest to work with you, if they don't understand WTF you're saying or whether you can help them get what they want?

You'll know you're stuck in Tool Town, or communicating a message that has no story substance or 3 P language when after you tell someone what you do, they say, "That's so cool/interesting" but they don't ask additional questions except out of obligation, and no one seems willing to invest.

Speak to the *pain, pleasure,* and *person* when you communicate with your audience, always. Tools are often helpful because they can add a compelling element to your message. For example, let's say that you do psychic readings and you let people know that you use tarot cards, tea leaves, crystals, or the human design modality. These are tools that might enhance your marketing message if they are a true aspect of your style that your audience is drawn to.

Let's take a look at an example of messaging that's chock full of the 3 Ps + tools that are compelling for your audience. Then we'll start gaining clarity about how you can identify your 3 Ps and use them to market your business. This messaging is from the back cover of my book *When Spirits Speak:*

Pain   Pleasure   Person   Tool

What would it mean to you to be able to use any one of the clair senses to speak to Spirit whenever you choose? What if you knew with confidence that you could accurately communicate life-changing and profoundly healing messages from anyone's passed loved ones?

One of the talents that Melissa Pharr brings to spiritual development is her ability to make the intangible work of mediumship more easily understood. She does this by using her never-before-seen, step-by-step Mediumship Development Framework, which every spiritual practitioner can understand. It focuses on the five aspects of mediumship mechanics and best practices that have helped her and her students progress as efficiently and quickly as possible.

Melissa Pharr divulges, in detail, her many mediumship hacks and secrets that so seldom are shared by mentors and in development circles. In these pages, you'll discover:

- How to prepare for your readings so that you feel confident in your skills and strongly connected to the spirits who come through.
- How to navigate a shit show reading that doesn't work out without having your confidence destroyed.
- Seven ways to handle pressure as a medium and keep a strong link with a spirit even when your sitter is difficult to read for.
- How to manage a reading with multiple spirits like a badass and deliver many impactful messages in one sitting.

And so much more!

If you're a developing medium wanting to strengthen your skills in the most effective, powerful, and FUN way, this book has way more than you've bargained for! If you feel your development has slowed or plateaued, or that you bring through the same old evidence in the same old ways, the teachings and exercises in this book will bust you out of your rut.

In the words of so many of her students, Mel genuinely cares about helping you become the best medium you can be. She holds nothing back and shares only enthusiasm and excitement for your progress.

Can you see how there's not much in this messaging that *isn't* one of the 3 Ps or a tool? That's because our audience has to receive the validation that they are a fit for our offers—especially the paid ones—over and over again before they feel comfortable enough to invest.

How do you create a 3 P + tools message of your own? This is where it gets super fun because we're going to craft your marketing message Mad Libs style. How? We're going to start by recalling and listing each P and tool. After that, I'll be sharing some powerful formulas to craft sexy bullets that will be magnetically attractive when you communicate with your audience.

I'll start by revisiting my list of tools from the table I shared with you when we discussed how to create your framework. If you haven't made your list yet, let mine inspire you to create your own list now that you'll be able to draw from once we put these all together.

Tools

- Sitting in the power
- Meditation

- Remote viewing
- Using and understanding spiritual files
- How to become a clear channel
- Exercises to handle hearing "no"
- How to increase your confidence as a medium
- Automatic writing
- How to find/develop a spiritual community
- How to calm your nerves with a physical cue
- Exercises to handle tricky sitters
- Creating spiritual boundaries
- How to work with multiple spirits
- Noticing sounds for clairaudient development
- How to give a spiritual assessment
- How to create symbols with Spirit
- How to identify a spirit
- Mediumship ethics
- The difference between psychic work and mediumistic work
- How to cycle through the clairs for better evidence

Now we'll list P for Person, P for Pain, and P for pleasure:

P for Person

- Woman
- Parent/Mother
- Kind-hearted
- Spiritually inclined
- Emotionally intelligent
- Therapist
- In her 40s
- Married
- Empathic

- Sensitive
- Humanitarian
- Has a son and daughter
- Average height, slim, brown hair, brown eyes

P for Pain

- Lost her sister/loved one
- Aging parents
- Takes on the emotions of others easily
- Struggles with her connection to Spirit at times
- Struggles to separate her emotions from other people's
- Isn't as accurate as she'd like with mediumship
- Didn't get to say goodbye to her sister
- Feels guilt because she didn't speak to her sister much before her sister died
- Feels that others don't always understand her sensitivity
- Can be a people pleaser to her own detriment
- Is sensitive to the state of the world
- Struggles with mediumship cycles
- Doesn't feel her evidence during a reading is specific enough
- Feels like she doesn't know how to blend strongly with Spirit
- Has spontaneous spiritual experiences but doesn't know how to use her clairs on demand

P for Pleasure

- To feel spiritually connected with her sister/passed loved one
- To feel peace about her parents and for them to be healthy
- To have healthier emotional boundaries
- To feel strongly connected to Spirit

- To be able to more easily separate her emotions from other people's
- To be more accurate as a medium
- To know that her sister knows she loves her
- To let go of guilt and make peace with the relationship she had with her sister when she was alive
- To accept and take ownership of her sensitivity
- To be able to do what's right for her guilt free
- To know how to care for herself when the world is overwhelming
- To trust Spirit when she goes through different mediumship cycles
- To get specific, jaw-dropping evidence when she gives readings
- To feel strongly connected with Spirit
- To develop her clair senses and learn the language of Spirit

Now that you've got your lists together, let me show you how using the 3 Ps + tools can command the attention of your ideal client using my Mad Lib style formulas! These formulas will help you to position yourself as an expert and communicate to your clients that you can help them overcome their struggles and achieve the results they want.

The So That You Can Strategy

The *So That You Can Strategy* is one of my favorite Mad Lib style formulas. It's brilliant for helping you remember to keep the client's pleasure point front and center. It looks like this:

I'll help you _____ so that you can _____ and _____.
           (Tool)   (Pleasure)   (Pleasure)

When you're using the *So That You Can Strategy*, it's great to insert two pleasure points.

One of the tools that I teach my clients is how to become a clear channel for Spirit. If I were to simply say, "I'll help you learn to become a clear channel for Spirit" that may not be enough to have someone think that what I offer is worth investing money in. But when I tack on the *So That You Can* formula, the message becomes much more compelling. Using my client's pleasure points and the tools I teach, I'll show the value of becoming a clear channel for Spirit:

Example:

> "I'll help you (learn to become a clear channel for Spirit)
> so that you can (become a more accurate medium,) and
> (get specific, jaw-dropping evidence.)

Using your lists of Ps and tools, try creating a few of your own *So That You Can* sentences.

Craft Great Titles for Video Content, Webinars, Lead Magnets, Social Posts, and Emails

Titles are a big deal. Titles stop an ideal client in their tracks and have them decide in less than three seconds whether it's worth spending their time paying attention to you. As you flesh out your yeses that make up the levels of your client pathway pyramid, there will be plenty of opportunities to use this title formula.

If you end up wanting more viewers on your live social media videos, title them. If you're looking to get higher conversions with your opt-ins and free content, make sure they have excellent titles. Looking for higher open rates for your emails and more comments on your social posts or blog? You know what to do. Give them exceptional titles that showcase the 3 Ps!

Fill in the Blank Title Formula

_____ _____ _____ to help you
(#)   (Adjective)   (Tool)

_____ and _____
(Pleasure)   (Pleasure)

(OPTIONAL) without _____ .
(Pain)

Example:

3 Easy Exercises to strengthen your
clairs and speak to Spirit
(without worrying that you're making it up!)

Using your lists of Ps and tools, try creating a few of your own
Fill in the Blank Title formulas.

The Bangin' Bullet Formula

After you've crafted that compelling title, you can share with your
audience what's in it for them. This will work in many places within
your messaging. You can use these bullets during a sales conversation, in a sales email, on a lead page for your opt-in, on a sales page
for your offer, during a live training/webinar when you make your
offer, etc.

The Bangin' Bullet Formula

_____ the _____ _____
(Compelling Verb)   (#)   (Adjective)

_____ to _____ and _____ .
(Tool)   (Pleasure)   (Pleasure)

Example:

Discover my top 3 simple and free
mediumship hacks to bring through quality evidence
and give highly accurate readings that are
life-changing for your sitter.

Using your lists of Ps and tools, try creating a few of your own *Bangin' Bullet* formulas.

So That You Can Bullet Formula

_____ _____ , so that you can
   (Compelling Verb)   (Tool)

_____ *and* _____ .
   (Pleasure)   (Pleasure)

Example:

Become masterful at working with multiple spirits at once
so that you can bring through more than one
passed loved one during a reading and match your
evidence with the right spirit.

Using your lists of Ps and tools, try creating a few of your own *So That You Can Bullet* formulas. If it helps, reference the lists below in terms of more numbers, compelling verbs, and adjectives that you can plug in as well.

Compelling Verb Examples

- Discover
- Learn
- Uncover
- Reveal
- Master
- Explore
- Identify
- Gain

Numbers

Odd numbers are great, like 3, 5, and 7. Smaller numbers, like 7 or less, work well because they may seem more doable. Don't be afraid to use other numbers, like dates, or statistics that support the goal of your messaging. Numbers in your marketing message give it a tangible feel and specificity that elevates what you have to say and makes it more interesting.

Adjective Examples

- Secret
- Simple
- Smart
- Sexy
- Amazing
- Awesome
- Best
- Bold
- Brilliant
- Clever
- Clear
- Concrete
- Costly
- Delicious
- Dazzling
- Essential
- Exciting
- Fabulous
- Fantastic
- Healthy
- High-level
- Important
- Juicy
- Magnificent
- Natural
- Necessary
- Powerful
- Practical
- Remarkable
- Spectacular
- Tragic
- Worthwhile

Bringing 3 P Language + Tools and Story Substance Together

A fantastic message utilizes both 3 P language + tools *and* story substance. The most compelling way to talk about what you do is to masterfully craft a message that first includes story substance. Your values, beliefs, and mission—although not spelled out directly every time you communicate with your ideal audience—are strongly illustrated within your words and story. They go straight to the heart of your audience. Your ideal clients are attracted to you because they share the same values, beliefs, and mission that you've expressed. They create a strong connection and bond, sometimes immediately, but definitely over time if you're consistent.

Your story should also be chock full of 3 P language. Not only does it connect deeply with your audience due to the powerful stories that you consciously include, but it *always* includes language that clearly, concisely, and quickly addresses the 3 Ps, and optionally includes compelling tools as well. Your clients are never confused about what's in it for them, because you always make it clear that you understand their struggles, and that you can help them overcome and reach their desired result. Your 3 Ps are specific and are targeted precisely to *your* ideal audience. At the end of the day you've just got to have a clear sign over your door to make sure that clients actually walk through it.

Lastly, it's a must to know the purpose of your post. It's important that you always know what the purpose is of any messaging that you put out there in the online world. Here's an example of messaging that I used for an email to my list about open enrollment for my development circle. It includes story substance and the 3 Ps + tools!

Purpose of the post = convert subscribers to development circle students

Pain

Pleasure

Story Substance is within { }

Hiya Subscriber First Name,

Do you ever wonder what you'd learn in my development circle?

{**In the latest round of my <u>Mediumship Development Circle</u> I remember a student of mine learning something extremely valuable during her first class.** She was giving a reading, and she identified the spirit as the sitter's passed cousin. The sitter said yes. **Shortly after,** the sitter started to say "no" to most of the evidence that my student was bringing through. *My student told me she felt stuck.*

I linked in to see how I might support my student. I sensed quickly that there were two spirit people present—both women during their lifetimes. While one was her cousin, the other felt like a close friend to me.

I asked my student, "Can you sense that there is more than one spirit present here?"

She paused for a moment, allowing herself to attune to the spiritual connection, and then frowned, "No, I can't tell."

"That's ok," I said, "You might still come to that conclusion by realizing that she started out with yeses but then switched to nos. That can often be a sign that your evidence is legit, but there's more than one spirit and you're attributing the evidence to the wrong spirit."

"So what do I do?" She asked.

"I would ask the sitter, 'Is it possible that the evidence I've brought through could match for another passed spirit who isn't your cousin?'"

She asked this question of her sitter, and her sitter said yes. Then my student began hearing yeses again, with consistency.}

I wasn't surprised when she immediately signed up for this round of development circle when enrollment opened.

If you'd like to see what you might learn during my class, there's a chance to try out a one-off development circle class for just $35 HERE.

But if you know that you want in, it's best to snag a seat in circle *now* because **enrollment is closing in less than a week and all three of my classes are nearly sold out.**

Enroll Here!

Plus, don't forget this two-part bonus that I added when you enroll in my Mediumship Development Circle.

Bonus Training Part 1: AN ENCORE Training Of

The Top 3 Mistakes Mediums Make when it comes to growing a business and actually making money &

The EXACT 3 things to focus on INSTEAD to make a living as a medium

During this training I'll lay out my current business model, plans for expansion, and estimated revenue for this year!

Bonus Training Part 2: Design Your 90-Day Business Profit Plan (*Training and Workshop for Mediums*)

There's no reason you can't make back the investment for this Mediumship Development Circle over a 90-day period if you implement what you'll learn in this training.

If you feel called, I so hope to see you in circle!

All my love,

Mel <3

P.S. Any questions? Just reply to this email. I'm happy to help!

P.P.S. Enrollment ends in less than a WEEK! *Enroll Here!*

Other Tips for Powerful Messaging

When you're sharing story substance in a message, make sure the story or story snippet you've shared checks these boxes below.

1. **Does it position you as an expert?** Does it showcase something you've mastered, completed, or achieved that your audience desires to achieve?
2. **Does it make you relatable and show that you are a human who can be vulnerable (in a positive way)?** What struggles have you overcome that your ideal client is facing?
3. **Does it showcase who you are as a mentor and leader?** What about you do others find compelling? Yes, you *are* interesting, so be interesting by figuring this one out!

4. **Does it demonstrate your confidence in your work?** People want to work with someone who believes in themselves. Even subconsciously, they know that you cannot believe in them if you don't believe in yourself.

5. **Does it feel genuine?** Keep it real. Be transparent. Be yourself. Focus less on trying to be like someone else or trying *not* to be like other people. Focus on being you.

6. **Does it have specific details that can't be replicated?** Your details make you different from everyone else. There's nothing worse than general statements.

(General and boring example) "I love helping my clients improve their mediumship so they can change lives!"

(Interesting example with details) "How do I teach differently than other mentors with development circles? I help my students develop their clair senses to a higher level of proficiency by having them isolate each clair over a period of classes.*

Here's an example.

Last week I had my clients use only clairgustance (clear tasting) and clairalience (clear smelling) to bring through evidence from a spirit. This helps them expand what I call their 'spiritual toolbox' with these two clairs.

Here's the feedback I got from one of my students the very next week.

Hi, Mel! I just wanted to share with you, and also to thank you(!) for another great class on Tuesday re: smell/taste. I gave a reading on Wednesday and asked the spirit to let me smell what I saw in the kitchen. Here is part of the sitter's feedback:

*"This was one of the best readings I've had in my life (I've had a lot). I loved how you described my grandma's essence perfectly. Specific information about her life, home, etc., and how she felt was 100% accurate. I could go on for paragraphs, **but when you could smell the pot roast cooking that was so amazing!"***

Mel, you are correct—sitters love this nugget! I was able to smell her very strong perfume as well!

Many thanks for guiding me in stepping up my game! Love it!

Linda

USING YOUR EXPERTISE AND FREE CONTENT TO CREATE A FOLLOWING

Now that you understand how to speak to your ideal audience in a way that shows your expertise and attracts them as interested prospects, you want to make sure that they have an easy and desirable option to officially join your community as a subscriber! Many entrepreneurs make this common mistake: they fail to create a direct communication avenue with followers, relying instead on platforms they don't control. For example, let's say that you relied heavily on a social media channel like TikTok to book readings. If something were to happen to that social media platform, and you hadn't created a way for prospects to move from TikTok to your email list, you'd be out of luck in terms of continuing to generate business.

This is why it's so important that you create a way of growing a list of potential clients who are likely to say yes to working with you.

It makes it much easier to create revenue consistently from month to month.

I'm going to share how to expand your following with free content that positions you as an expert and gives interested people a high-quality sample of what you do. This will help you to build trust within your growing community and move them closer to saying yes to the transformation they desire with your support.

Creating free content (aka freebies, opt ins, lead magnets, etc.) is not just a way to attract an audience. It's also a way to nurture your audience, *and* make an invitation! We'll dive deeper into nurturing our audience and making invitations in upcoming chapters. Our primary focus at this point is to create a free offer that's compelling and helpful enough to convert our ideal audience into regular subscribers. If it's a juicy enough Free Easy Yes and strategically placed and shared, it can make growing your following a constant and consistent thing. *This* is the ultimate goal.

To do this we'll be focusing on two aspects of using free content to grow your spiritual community. The first is creating content that's congruent with your client pathway pyramid. It's very important that what you create makes sense in the larger picture of your client pathway pyramid that you're looking to design. We'll take a look at how to generate content that supports offers you'll make down the road and further develops your brand and the work you'd like to be known for. It'll be helpful to check in with your audience once again (or at least refer to the market research you've already done) to make sure you're creating content that will attract the right followers. We're looking for that perfect intersection of what you love doing best, and what your audience needs and desires *most*.

The second is mapping out your free content. I'm excited to share with you a step-by-step process for designing free content that's high quality and also helps to wow your new followers so that they're more likely to stick around and potentially convert into paying clients. We'll dive into the details of how to get your free content out there once we've gone through the process of creating it.

If you're at a stage of business where you've already got great free content that converts followers to subscribers (aka a lead magnet or opt-in), or many, you can use what I'll be sharing to make any necessary improvements to your current content. You also have the option to create something brand new now if you've been inspired by all of your tools and topics that you've listed in your framework.

Trust me when I say that it's less about how much content you create to attract subscribers and more about creating content that is aligned with a greater marketing strategy. That means that what you put out is congruent with your Client Pathway Pyramid *and* it's content that you genuinely love to share because it feels like a true extension of what you do best.

People love content that effectively and efficiently helps them solve their problems. Most humans aren't patient, so share a simple piece of what you do to help them start to solve their problems and get results quickly; you'll develop a following over time no doubt. The best thing is, your free content gets to win them over, instead of you feeling like you've got to hunt down clients and convince them that you've got value to offer and that they should work with you.

If what you put out for free is super high quality, your peeps will be more inclined to know, like, and trust you. Your goal might be to hear your prospects say: "If her free stuff is this good, I can't wait to see how amazing that offer she's launching is. I'm in!" Prime them to invest by building a relationship with them that starts with you being generous, honest, full of integrity, and sharing with them something that's so good, they'd likely pay for it. I knew it was time for me to go pro when I was giving free mediumistic readings and my sitters started to ask if they could pay me or donate. One woman said to me after the reading, "I would gladly pay $100s for this. It was a life-changing experience. You need to start charging."

Before we start part one by creating content that's congruent with your Client Pathway Pyramid, I'd like to point out that this is also the time to set up a couple of technical things in your business. The first is your Customer Relations Management software, or CRM, as we call it in the online marketing world. Because we want to have those who are exposed to our work subscribe to our email list, we'll need to set up a CRM so that we have a system to email them with. With this system, when you share your free content, ideal leads can opt in and get added to your list. In addition, as soon as you have ideal clients on your list, you'll want to be emailing them regularly, even if it's just once a week, to build a genuine relationship. For online entrepreneurs who are in the beginning stages, I recommend something like AWeber or Mailchimp because they have free or financially accessible plans. Software like Ontraport, Infusionsoft, and Active Campaign are also options, but in exchange for having more capabilities, they are more expensive.

If you're severely technically challenged and you have a small budget to spend, consider hiring a virtual assistant to get things set up for you. There's a little backend work that'll go into the process like designing a lead page (a page that illustrates the benefits of opting into an email list in return for your free content) and integrating it with your CRM system, etc. If you feel ready, and finally financially able, please God hire someone. I promise you, you'll say to yourself in a cheery voice, "I'll just design my own lead page to save some money!" Three hours to three months later you'll say, "I fucking hate lead pages. I have no idea how to integrate this with my email system. I want to break my computer." It won't be in a cheery voice either. I pulled my hair out one too many times trying to do many of the things that web designers, FB ad experts, and virtual assistants (VAs) can do better for a relatively small amount of money in a fraction of the time. I thought I was saving time and money by doing these things myself, but really, I was wasting it. I most definitely wasn't focusing on things that *could* have been getting me clients.

You don't need to spend an arm and a leg having a VA working with you full-time if you're not there yet. Bringing someone awesome on for one or two simple projects is most definitely a possibility.

P.S. look for a freelancer with great reviews on upwork.com or fiverr.com. The amount of time and stress you'll save is well worth the cost of paying someone anywhere from $15 - $50/hour to have your opt-in set up go smoothly.

It's *so* very important that the free content you create makes sense in the larger picture of your client pathway pyramid. That means that you create content that will attract leads who will likely be interested in your paid offers down the road.

Your free content is a Free Easy Yes. It will likely be one of the first Free Easy Yeses that your new follower sees from you and what begins them on the path to saying yes to a low to medium price point offer and/or a higher price point offer. With this in mind, can you see how your lead magnet or opt-in is a powerful opportunity to wow your prospect? It's your chance to overdeliver so that you can build trust and create a relationship where you're the expert to help them create the transformation they desire.

There are three things we'll be revisiting to create free content that is congruent with your Client Pathway Pyramid. The first is your Client Pathway Pyramid.

CLIENT PATHWAY PYRAMID

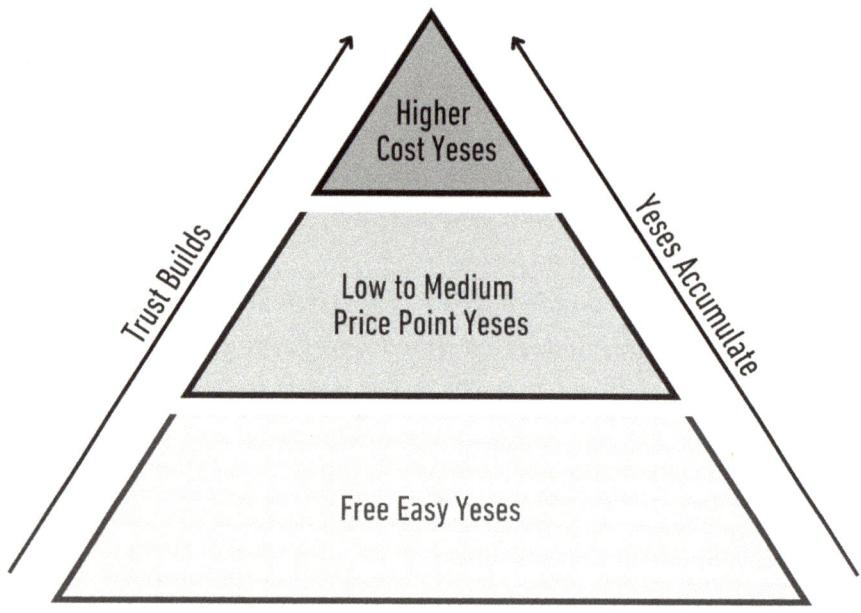

Now you're going to add in your "Just Starting" or "For the Future" offer(s) that you ultimately want your free content to lead to. That means that as you create your free content, you're consciously deciding which offer is most important for you to sell at the moment based on your business revenue and impact goals.

I remember when I wanted to sell my sales course, *Master Your Money Conversations* back in the day. I created free content that attracted the *perfect* person who would be interested in my course. It was called, *The Top 10 Ways to Book 20+ Sales Calls a Month*. It was my best performing free content because the title was so specific, pinpointing both the pain and pleasure points of my ideal client. The majority of people who signed up for my course had joined my list from that opt-in.

Currently, I've created free content called *3 Easy Exercises to Strengthen Your Clairs and Speak to Spirit,* that attracts an ideal client who will be interested in almost all of my offers. This is what happens when you've become very specific about exactly who you want to attract. The diagram below of my Client Pathway Pyramid includes both my "Just Starting" and "For the Future" offers.

CLIENT PATHWAY PYRAMID
(WITH OFFERS)

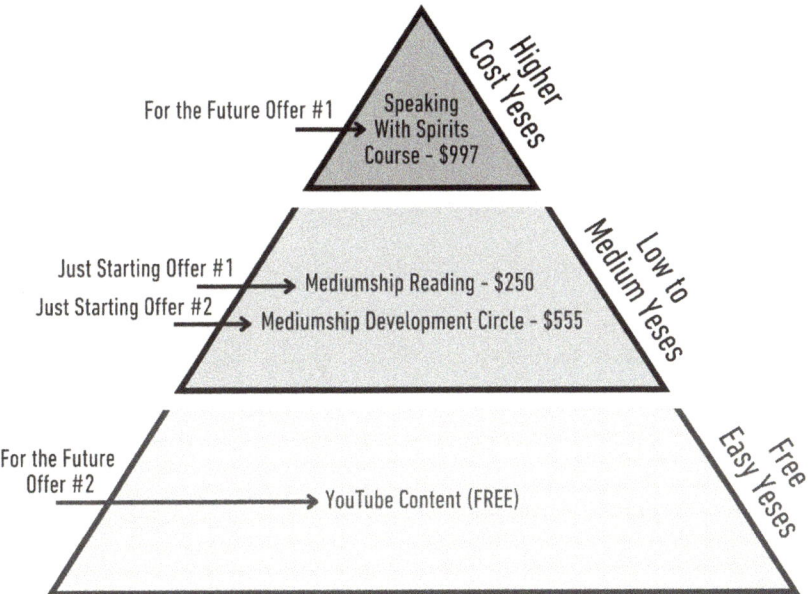

Add the paid offer or offers that you're focusing on right now into your Client Pathway Pyramid. Decide which offer is most important to you to validate and sell at the moment. For me, it's important that I'm creating free content that attracts ideal clients who will likely be interested in both my mediumship course, *Speaking With Spirits,* and my mediumship development circle.

Now that I'm clear on my ultimate business goal in terms of what offer(s) I want to sell, it's time to pin the tail on the donkey, baby. That's right, you could literally blindfold yourself and point to the sexy framework that you've just created. Did your finger land on an overarching step or tool that you can turn into free content to attract someone who might be the perfect fit for your offer? Go ahead. Look at your framework right now. It will give you plenty of ideas about what content you can create that is congruent with your client pathway and that leads straight to your paid offer(s).

Remember that the first thing to do is to decide what offer is most important for you to focus on and sell. Because I'll be focusing on my *Speaking With Spirits* course and my development circle, both of which are about helping my clients get results, I'm going to showcase my Client Results Framework on the following page. Everything in one of the boxes are the kinds of things that my ideal client is begging me for help with on a regular basis. Which one feels like the *most* important one for them? Which one is drool-worthy and will do a fantastic job of getting them through the door? Ultimately, my goal is to have the honor of helping them develop as a highly proficient medium.

Next, you'll want to decide upon a step or tool that you could create free content from. Remember *The Top 10 Ways To Book 20+ Sales Calls A Month*? So drool-worthy right? What would that be for your ideal potential clients? Take a look at each overarching step or tool. Think about what your ideal clients tend to ask the most questions about. What is the most common question you get? If you don't have any clients of your own yet, reflect upon your own FAQs that you had when you were first developing your mediumship.

Step 1	Step 2	Step 3	Step 4	Step 5
Clear Channel	*Communication and the Clairs*	*Confidence*	*Community*	*Command of Craft*
Sitting in the power	Remote viewing (Clairvoyance)	Exercises to handle hearing "no"	How to find/develop a spiritual community	Using and understanding spiritual files
Meditation	Automatic writing (Claircognizance)	How to increase your confidence as a medium	How to find a good mediumship mentor	Creating spiritual boundaries
Decluttering	Noticing sounds (Clairaudience)	How to calm your nerves with a physical cue	How to find a good development circle	How to work with multiple spirits
Taking care of your physical health	How to identify a spirit (multiple clairs)	Exercises to handle tricky sitters		How to give a spiritual assessment
	Cycling the clairs (multiple clairs)			Creating symbols with Spirit
				Mediumship ethics
				The difference between psychic and mediumistic work

As I looked at this framework for the first time, step two really jumped out at me. I realized that it was compelling for a lot of my ideal clients to want to strengthen their clair senses. In fact, over email and in response to my YouTube videos via the comments, I constantly was getting asked how to "strengthen" or "develop" a particular clair. More often, someone would ask me how to strengthen all of them.

Now that I've chosen the topics of strengthening your clairs, there are a few things I want to keep in mind to make sure I'm playing a longer and more impactful game.

At this point, you'll want to check in and ask yourself if your free content is congruent with your client pathway pyramid. Does your content topic attract followers who may say yes to the offers you're wanting to prioritize and then make it likely that they'll flow through your client pathway pyramid? Additionally, does this topic gel with who you are and give you opportunities to share stories with substance that will resonate with your ideal audience? The answer for me is a definite yes. My ideal clients want to become proficient mediums and strengthening their clairs is an absolute must. For my Free Easy Yeses to my low, medium and high price point offers, the clairs will be an important throughline. It's so important to get this right. If you were to create something that isn't congruent, then it likely won't attract your ideal client, and even if it does, they may not flow through to your paid offers in your client pathway. A silly example of getting this wrong that I like to share and nerd out about? Imagine creating free content about how to fix your lawn mower. Clearly this will attract people who are not your ideal clients. There's also a slim to none chance that they will invest in your paid offers and honey, slim just left town.

The other thing I check in with myself about is whether my free content is something I'm passionate about and good at helping others with. You want your free content to be something that you're good at delivering and passionate about so that you can overdeliver and create that wow-factor for subscribers. For me, being passionate about what I teach is always an easy yes. In addition, I use all of the clairs in my work and love practicing exercises to strengthen my clairs. Teaching this is fun for me and I have endless ways to help my clients with their clair senses.

When it comes to creating free content to grow your audience, the best lead magnets offer transformation, tools, and learning that your ideal leads will want so badly, they'll likely pay money for it, let alone say yes to free content. Ask yourself if your free content is something your ideal audience craves. Remember that I thought back to the most common FAQs that I encounter because this tells me what my clients are the most interested in within my CRF. We'll discuss revisiting your clients' survey results next in this chapter.

Focus your free content on a part of your Client Results Framework that your ideal clients are conscious of desiring, and needing, in order to achieve the results they ultimately want at the end of the day. Cold leads don't know you, so trying to educate or convince them about needing a piece of your expertise never works as well. Instead, you want to create free content that they are already hungry for. The great news? My clients already crave help with their clairs. They understand the importance without education from me. This makes my free content and exercises immediately valuable to them.

2) Mapping out your free content

Now that you've put some good thought into what topic you'll focus on to create your lead magnet, it's time to design the content. Below, I'm sharing with you a step-by-step process that'll help you simplify mapping out your free content. After that, we'll dive into how you can market your free content to grow your list and nurture your audience.

As you move forward with this process, take some time to listen in. Don't forget to allow your originality to pour through. Reflect on the journey that you've taken and your own beliefs and values and will likely resonate with your ideal clients. Include these things in your teachings to continue to develop your own voice and speak to your audience on an even deeper level as you deliver value.

I suggest keeping your content simple and step-by-step, which will be easy to do with the process that I've outlined below. It's so important to make sure that your prospects can digest it easily and get value quickly. The sooner they see that you've got something powerful to offer, the more time they'll spend in your community, and hopefully as a paid client!

1) Survey your audience or revisit your previous survey results + title your free content.

Don't skimp here! Survey your audience about the content you're planning to create. If you've already done surveys and the results support your topic, revisit those findings. Either way, you need audience validation before moving forward. You want to make sure that what you create is actually something that they really want. While it may be free, downloading free content in exchange becoming a subscriber is not something that most people do easily these days. Most people want *less* emails in their inbox and they only pay attention to those things that are quickly and effectively addressing their Ps. You also want to be able to hear their *exact* language and then use their words in the title you choose for your free content. Your ideal clients should feel like you're reading their mind and knowing exactly what they want. When I look back at how my ideal clients responded during my initial surveys, many of them said the phrase "strengthen my clairs" and that they wanted to get better at "giving readings" and "communicating with Spirit." It's precisely why I used the formula below that I shared with you earlier, and gave my working lead magnet the title, *3 easy exercises to strengthen your clairs and speak to Spirit.*

Fill in the Blank Title Formula

_____ _____ _____ to help you
(#)   (Adjective)   (Tool)

_____ and _____
(Pleasure)   (Pleasure)

(OPTIONAL) without _____ .
(Pain)

Once you've got your content idea and you've given it a 3 P title and written 3-5 bullets that you think are compelling, ask your ideal clients if they love your topic and title. You can:

- **Post on social media** and have them rate first the topic and then the title on a scale of 1-10. 1 being the lowest score and 10 being the highest.
- **Email your list** if you have one. I simply let them know the topic and title I'm thinking about and ask if there is something different they want or if they like my idea, and why.
- **Reach out personally to past and current clients.** Anyone you've worked with who feels like a member of your ideal audience is worth getting feedback from.
- **Pay close attention to what your ideal clients seem to be struggling with the most, and most often.** This can be as easy as doing some online research among the audience of

other leaders in your industry if you don't have your own audience yet.

If it turns out that your audience isn't as excited about this content topic as you thought, revisit their pain and pleasure points. Head back to your framework to choose another step or topic that you think they *will* crave and start the survey process over.

2) Know the purpose of your free content.

This is a simple question for you to be clear on. You'll want to know the answer *before* you create your free content. Once they consume it, what should they be able to do, or have learned or achieved? It's a bit like a mini point A to point B, like we did to begin the process of creating your framework.

3) Reverse engineer your process.

It can be as simple as looking back on how *you* were able to do what your lead magnet will help your ideal client do. Think back to each step that you took to have this result, and map it out. It'll make the process easy for your client to follow, and it'll make it yours by bringing your own unique style to your own original how-to process.

This will be similar to when you were creating your framework, except now it'll be a smaller or mini framework with the specific purpose from step two. Another option to consider instead of steps, might be to think of exercises that you could include that will help clients create the result they want. For example, in my free content, I give them three easy exercises that will help them strengthen their clair senses.

Whether exercises or education, map out your overarching steps or exercises. Second, think of pointers or tips that will help your prospect master each. It's always helpful as you follow this process to ask yourself, "How did I create this result?"

I suggest creating no more than three to five steps or exercises. You may be able to refer back to your CRF to help with these steps, but not necessarily. Many times, the steps of your free content will be much more micro than what you've included in your CRF or CEF. It's important to keep it easy to follow and quick to receive value to ensure that your potential client actually consumes your free offer and is more likely to get great results from it. This makes it more likely that you'll turn a follower into a raving fan and a prospect who may eventually invest with you. You can organize your content in the way I've shown below to map it out, extending to five steps or exercises if it's really necessary and helps your subscriber get quick results. Once you've got the steps or exercises in place, flesh out each one with one to three pointers to help make it easier for them to get results fast and avoid any common mistakes.

- **Step 1:**
  - Pointer 1:
  - Pointer 2:
  - Pointer 3:
- **Step 2:**
  - Pointer 1:
  - Pointer 2:
  - Pointer 3:
- **Step 3:**
  - Pointer 1:
  - Pointer 2:
  - Pointer 3:

4) Add in impressive stats, client testimonials, and/story elements.

These details provide proof of your expertise and how well your content, and what you teach, kicks buns. For example, with my three easy exercises free content, I can easily share a story about teaching one of the exercises during my course, *Speaking With Spirits.* I can share that I received an email from a client about how well they started to do in their readings after these exercises and that they were thrilled to be getting more specific and accurate evidence.

5) Presenting your free content.

Now that you've got your content mapped out, it's a good idea to know how you plan to deliver it to your ideal clients. As I've shared previously, it's important to think about the delivery of your free content and how it's going to create an experience for your ideal client. You've likely seen all kinds of possibilities for free content. Sometimes free content is presented as a video training, PDF module, quiz, or even a template or checklist. Because I want to create more of an experience and build trust quickly, I love to create training videos that are accompanied by a PDF style report or module.

Regardless of where you choose to share this free content to convert followers to subscribers, you'll want to have a landing page or lead page where followers can opt-in. You can use tools like leadpages.net, unbounce.com, or instapage.com that integrate with your CRM to do this. A lead page or landing page always has a title, some bullets that describe what's in it for your subscribers, a place for them to enter their name and email to join your list and receive your free offer, and a bio. If you can, it's best to include some testimonials or social proof as well. Just a note that this is different from creating your website, which we will get to by the end of this chapter. For now, I always suggest creating a simple landing page to start. This allows you to start pulling the attract lever as soon as possible without the stress of having an entire website completed.

You can use this formula below to help with the creation of your title:

Fill in the Blank Title Formula

_____ _____ _____ to help you
(#)   (Adjective)   (Tool)

_____ and _____ .
(Pleasure)   (Pleasure)

You can also revisit the following formulas with examples to create some compelling bullets on your landing page or lead page to share with your audience what's in it for them:

Fill in the Blank Bullet Formula

_____ the _____ _____
(Compelling Verb)   (#)   (Adjective)

_____ to _____ and _____ .
(Tool)   (Pleasure)   (Pleasure)

Example:

Discover my top 3 simple and free
mediumship hacks to bring through quality evidence
and give highly accurate readings that are
life-changing for your sitter.

So That You Can Bullet Formula

_____ _____ , so that you can
(Compelling Verb)   (Tool)

_____ *and* _____ .
(Pleasure)   (Pleasure)

Example:

> Become masterful at working with multiple spirits at once so that you can bring through more than one passed loved one during a reading and match your evidence with the right spirit.

Lastly, you can think about a story that illustrates your point and gives credibility to your offer to make it even more desirable. This is the part where I might share the story of a current student of mine who, after completing these exercises, started getting rave reviews from other mediums for her practice readings. When you pull all of these things together, you create a powerful way of presenting your free content to your ideal audience. Just to make it a bit easier for you, I've also included a checklist below:

Lead Page Checklist:

- Title
- Bullets (What you'll learn/get)
- Pain, Pleasure, Benefits
- Button (Sign Up! Make sure it appears on the page before they have to scroll down)
- Story Substance
- Privacy Policy
- Disclaimer

Optional:

- Picture of you
- Short Blurb/Bio about you
- Testimonials/Social Proof

You can see the example of my lead page that I use as one of my main opt-ins here:

https://www.mediumshipwithmel.com/3ee

6) You'll need a thank you page, thank you email, and a URL.

Once your new subscriber has opted in for your free content, you'll need a pop-up thank you page. This page will let them know that your free offer is awaiting them in their inbox. Keep in mind that a thank you page is valuable real estate. It's a great idea to put an invitation to follow you on other platforms to encourage interaction with you.

A thank you email should automatically go out when they opt in and deliver to them your free offer. This can be a simple email with a testimonial to remind them of the value of your free offer. We do this to increase the chances that they will actually consume it— only 30% of the people who download free content actually use it.

You're almost done! The last thing you need is to decide upon the URL for your offer. Don't make it difficult because it really doesn't matter what you choose as long as it's super simple. My rule is that I always choose a URL that's easy enough for someone to remember, even though that's not common these days with QR codes. Regardless, you want it to be easy to access like mine: https://www.mediumshipwithmel.com/3ee

YOUR ATTRACTION PLATFORM(S)

Before we get into this next step of being visible, we have to discuss how scary going public can be for some mediums. If you've felt or currently feel very nervous to come out as a medium, you aren't alone. When I began working with students in my development circle, I offered a bonus business training. Every time I gave a bonus training, students mentioned the fear of calling themselves a medium and letting people publicly know that this is something they practice professionally. The fact is that for many people, it's a big deal. Not everyone is surrounded by friends and family who are supportive and who understand mediumship. Even when you do have a supportive handful of people in your life, that doesn't guarantee that those people truly understand what it's like to do this work, let alone decide to give it a go as a pro. Many of us have to work through at least a little bit of fear or anxiety when we decide to let the people in our life know what we're up to. My previous career as an online marketing strategist helped me get used to marketing myself publicly and to overcome the initial emotions that come with online trolls. Still, letting those who are closer to you know that you're a medium can be a lot more nerve-wracking than when a stranger disapproves of your work. If you resonate with what I've shared, then I've got a few things you might try to work through your anxiety and fear.

Be clear and confident about your own positive motivations. When people feel averse or threatened by something, it's often because they don't understand it. When they respond poorly, it may be due to fear, even if that fear is unconscious. We don't need to get too nitty gritty into the psychology of it to understand the concept that humans fear what they don't understand. If you're able to be clear and confident about your own positive motivations for doing this work for good, it'll be easier for you to communicate them in a way that the people in your life can more easily understand. When you aren't sure about the why behind your work, you'll feel less confident sharing this path with others.

Find a community or friend for support. I went through the initial part of my mediumship journey without a medium friend or mediumship community. Luckily, I had plenty of friends who were spiritually open and excited about my new endeavors. My husband and parents were incredibly supportive as well. Still, there were many moments where I felt alone and isolated. As wonderful as these people were, they didn't really understand what it was like to *be* a medium. What I really yearned for was someone to talk to who was having similar experiences, or who at least knew what I was talking about and didn't think of mediumship as a wild and strange thing.

Thank Spirit that I went to study at Arthur Findlay College shortly after I became aware of my mediumistic abilities. My first week at Arthur Findlay College was one of the best weeks of my life, and the friends I met and the community I created there were full of incredible people who I still talk to on a regular basis. One of them in particular is a friend who I text with every single week. I can't tell you how many times we've discussed our unfolding abilities, our wins, and our shitshow readings that happen every once and again. We've cheered each other on countless times, encouraged each other when we're down, and simply enjoyed feeling like normal people together because we can talk about our work without having to feel like we're censoring ourselves or having to explain. We've also practiced mediumship exercises together, referred clients to each other, and introduced each other to more medium friends.

To me and to so many of my students, these friendships and a mediumship community are priceless. We don't always notice just how powerful this kind of support is while we have it, but your friend or community might be the reason you have the confidence to give a great reading when the one before was an absolute struggle. Or you might be the friend who helps someone find a perspective that keeps them in the game. My mediumship bestie found us the best mediumship class I'd ever taken, and we flew to the event and spent the week learning together. It became one more week of doing what I love that I'll never forget.

There are many places you could go to find mediumship friends and other fellow spiritual practitioners. Do some research about a couple of the opportunities in your area listed below and plan over the next month or 90 days to experience these environments and see how it goes!

- Mediumship conferences or events
- Mediumship classes online
- Spiritual meetups (try meetup.com in your area)
- Spiritualist churches
- Meditation circles
- Women's circles
- Men's circles
- Spiritual retreats
- Start your own mediumship community

I have yet to meet anyone who is strongly and passionately drawn to mediumship for no important reason. In my experience, everyone who feels pulled to speaking with Spirit feels that pull because they are meant to experience this work. I won't pretend that I always know what that reason is, but I've met plenty of people who will *never* have an interest in this work to know that those of us who do are meant to experience mediumship for a significant reason. With this in mind, trust your journey. You might give a reading or develop spiritual skills that create a life-changing experience for someone. Most definitely, mediumship will change your life for the better.

Now that we've got that out of the way, let's focus on figuring out where your people hang out. This could absolutely be online, but it doesn't have to be. Revisit your survey and see if you've managed to garner any information about what social media platforms your ideal clients are on, what books or magazines they read, what podcasts they listen to, and perhaps what other kinds of products or services they invest in. If you didn't manage to get much from them about those topics, now is the time to follow up with them. Below I've shared examples of what information is helpful to know about your ideal audience and some example questions as well. Keep in mind that these questions will only be helpful if they are asked in connection to your work. For example, you'll notice that the first question I listed is *"What books and/or magazines do you read that have to do with mediumship or spirituality?"* If I were to ask *"What books or magazines do you like to read?"* they could tell me about the latest novel they read and loved but it wouldn't do much to help me understand more about where and how they spend their time in a way that relates to mediumship.

- **Books and magazines they read and what podcast they listen to**
  - Example question: *"What books and/or magazines do you read that have to do with mediumship or spirituality?"*
  - Example question: *"What podcasts do you listen to that have to do with mediumship or spirituality?"*
- **Other practitioners, services, or products they invest in**
  - Example question: *"What other practitioners or services do you invest in that are in any way related to mediumship and the healing aspect of it? For example, do you see an energy healer, a therapist, or even a practitioner like a chiropractor?"*

- ○ Example question: *"Are there any products that you invest in that have any connection to spirituality or mediumship? Sometimes my clients buy books, crystals, spiritual decks, etc. Does this apply to you or help you think of products you enjoy?"*
- **Social media platforms they frequent**
  - ○ Example question: *"What social media platforms do you use?"*
  - ○ Example question: *"When you're on that social media platform what is your main goal? Are you looking to be social? Are you looking to buy something?"*
  - ○ Example question: *"Have you ever hired someone you came across on social media? What would you need the circumstance to be to trust and hire someone in this context?"*
- **Other mediums or spiritual practitioners that they follow and where**
  - ○ Example question: *"What other spiritual leaders, mediums, psychics do you follow?"*
  - ○ Example question: *"Where do you follow them and consume their content or come into contact with them?"*
- **Who they ask for a referral from when it comes to anything spiritual or relating to mediumship**
  - ○ Example question: *"If you wanted to hire a medium would you ask for a referral from someone you trust?"*
  - ○ Example question: *"If you were to hire a medium who would you ask for a referral from?"*

Once you learn this information from your ideal clients, make a list of all of the ways that you might be able to connect with them. It might look something like this list I've shared below.

All of the places I might connect with my ideal clients

- Next Level Soul podcast
- The Dead Life podcast
- Chiropractor
- Therapist
- Energy worker
- Books and spiritual decks
- YouTube
- TikTok
- Instagram
- John Edward
- Theresa Caputo
- Tyler Henry
- Laura Lynne Jackson
- Online reviews
- Ask friends who are mediums
- Ask close family friends

Your survey responses will give you all kinds of information and ideas about how you might start to consistently come into contact with ideal clients. It's important that you keep an open mind about the strategies you might use from the list you've created. For example, you'll see that I've brainstormed about how to find my ideal clients using the same list again.

All of the places I might connect with my ideal clients

- Next Level Soul podcast
  - It's a long shot but try to get interviewed on this podcast.
- The Dead Life podcast
  - It's a long shot but try to get interviewed on this podcast.
- Chiropractor

- ○ My chiro and many of the staff have had a reading with me. She also hosts large events. I should run the idea by her of being a referral partner and also of speaking on her stage at some point.
- Therapist
  - ○ I have a therapist who currently refers clients to me. I could seek out more.
- Energy worker
  - ○ I have an energy worker but I don't think she'd be interested in referring, but I could seek out others.
- Books and spiritual decks
  - ○ I'm at the stage of business where I've published two books and I'll be publishing my spiritual deck. I'll put QR codes in all of these that lead to a social platform and offer ideal clients to subscribe to my list.
- YouTube
  - ○ I love generating content. I love being on video. I'm disciplined and consistent. I think this will be a great platform for me.
- TikTok
  - ○ You couldn't fu**ing pay me to be on this platform.
- Instagram
  - ○ I'm ok with Instagram as long as I don't have to post more than two times a week. I'm not willing to be that person who posts stories constantly.
- John Edward
- Theresa Caputo
- Tyler Henry
- Laura Lynne Jackson
  - ○ For all of these celebrity mediums I could follow them online and engage with their subscribers in a genuine way to understand my ideal audience better.

- Online reviews
  - It would be good to get google reviews and yelp reviews… hmmm.
- Ask friends who are mediums
  - Definitely a referral system seems like a great way to go.
- Ask close family friends
  - Definitely a referral system seems like a great way to go.

As you can see, I've got all kinds of ideas about how to go about connecting with my audience, but I may not have the bandwidth to pursue all of them. In addition, I have to ask myself this important question: *What feels enjoyable and sustainable to me? What really fits well with who I am and what my skills are?*

I'm prolific when it comes to content creation. I like being on video and I don't like to feel tied to social media. Knowing these things about myself makes it easier for me to feel into the things on this list that feel enjoyable and creatively and energetically sustainable to me for the long haul.

Additionally, if I've learned anything over the years as an online marketing strategist, it's that spreading yourself too thin is not sustainable. I've seen too many entrepreneurs set up shop and fail because they are speaking to everyone and therefore, attracting no one.

It's sad, but a past client of mine from my marketing days had a vague self-help message that they marketed to anyone or thing that breathed. It sounded a bit like this, "If you want to become clear, I'm the perfect coach for you." Needless to say, her person as well as her pain and pleasure points weren't nearly specific enough.

I've also seen students do a little bit of everything to attract an audience and therefore become a master of none. This leads to failing at using *any* traffic source effectively. I remember a coaching call that I had with a client. She was in tears when we got on the phone because her social media calendar was causing her a disgusting amount of stress. She was on Facebook, Instagram, Periscope (do you remember that platform?!), Twitter, LinkedIn, and likely one or two more platforms. She didn't have the time she needed to be pulling the attract, nurture, and invite levers that would have taken a lot less time and been much more successful in getting her clients.

Unless you have all of the time and energy in the world, you'll need to select only one to three strategies for generating traffic. I've shared the list again a final time below to show you just how many ideas I cut—even just temporarily— in my first two years of business. In fact, the three places I chose to focus on to connect with my ideal clients easily enabled me to create a six-figure business and can easily sustain a multi-six or even seven-figure business. My areas of focus—YouTube, Instagram, and Referrals/Word of Mouth —should be familiar from Chapter 4 where I showcased my way of attracting an audience and my friend's way of attracting an audience.

Once you feel confident about where your ideal clients hang out and what suits you best, it's time to make the final decision about the one, two, or three places that you'll connect with potential clients. You can do what I've done and start crossing things out on your list to narrow it down. Remember that nothing is written in stone and you can always change up your strategy if you find that what you're doing isn't effective.

A word of caution though. Creating an audience that is genuinely interested in what you have to offer and who truly know, like, and trust you takes time. It's not an overnight thing. Never purchase leads and remember that these are real humans, not just numbers on your list. In the following chapters, we'll be discussing how to nurture your audience with care and invite them to engage with you in a meaningful way. For now, make a plan and stick to it. I don't recommend switching up your strategy until you've really given it all you've got for a good six months at the very least. While some people have referral programs or a social media following that blows up quickly, for most, attracting legit leads takes time. That's why it's never too soon to start.

DESIGNING YOUR WEBSITE TO ATTRACT IDEAL CLIENTS

We've arrived at that place that every new entrepreneur wants to dive into first thing. Yes, it's time to put your energy into a simple and effective website. That said, this is *not* a free pass to spend hours upon hours tweaking your website or trying to get it perfect because it doesn't need to be. Remember that it's *not* a client-getting activity to put your website together because it's not considered one of the five parts of the Client Attraction Framework. It is important, however, for your leads to have a place to go when they want to get more information about you and sign up to become a paying client. Now that you've come this far and you have clarity and ways to convert your leads to subscribers, it makes sense to put the time in.

Mark my words when I say, spend *no more* than 45 minutes a weekday on your site, if that. I want you to be doing money making activities right now and this is not one of them. I highly suggest keeping your website as simple as I've outlined it in this chapter. Clutter free, clean websites are the ones that do best.

Let's talk about some overarching things to keep in mind. First off, it's important to have at least one or two pictures that look professional. Maybe you have a friend who has a knack for taking pics that look just right. Or maybe you're ready to spend a little money with a photographer to create the look that you want for your About Me page. You decide, but have at least one or two pictures that look professional.

Next, make sure that all of the fonts you use are *legible.* It's great to find a cool style that you love and that captures your emerging brand. It's even better to make sure that the text you have on your site is easy to read. Remember that the confused customer doesn't buy or take you up on any of your calls to action.

Lastly, veto any long-winded writing! If you check out the sites of well-known mediums like Laura Lynne Jackson, Matt Fraser, Theresa Caputo, or Suzanne Giesemann, you'll notice that these sites get to the point quickly. I don't suggest making your site as complicated as theirs are in terms of all of their offers, media, and books. Remember that they've been at this for some time. I *do* suggest making your site simple and easy to navigate. These are the aesthetic boxes that you want to tick as you put your website together:

- Professional looking picture(s)
- Legible fonts
- Simple, clean, and easy to navigate pages

The Five Pages That Really Matter

I'm a huge fan of keeping your website simple. You want to make sure that it's easy to navigate. Your followers will browse and check out more of what you've got if they don't feel overwhelmed. You can always add more in the future. Remember that marketing yourself by taking client-getting actions is what's going to help you create an impact and revenue, not your website on its own. I'm listing the five pages that really matter below and then we'll dive deeper into constructing them.

- **Home Page**: Where they land that clearly and quickly conveys what you're all about. Think 3 Ps!
- **About Page:** This is the place to share your story in a way that positions you as an expert and resonates with your audience.

- **Services Page**: This is where ideal clients come to see their options for working with you. Depending on your offer(s), sales pages may be necessary and 3 P language is a must.
- **Contact Page**: This is a short and simple page that allows them to contact you via a web form.
- **Testimonial/Client Praise Page:** Here's where you can share the rave reviews from your clients that will help build trust with your followers who haven't experienced your work yet.

Other things you'll need:

- **Call to action**: You'll use your free content as an incentive for browsers to join your subscriber list.
- **Professional picture(s)**: As mentioned, professional pictures, even stock photos give it a polished feel.
- **Banner**: When someone comes to your site, your banner gives that first impression. This is so easy to do on a site like Squarespace. If you don't want to use a picture of yourself you can get a free or low-cost stock photo that gives prospects a feel for your work.

You might start by doing a little research and checking out sites that turn you on. These sites don't have to be the sites of other spiritual practitioners either. They could be companies or entrepreneurs that you like and respect, or sites that give a feel that resonates with you and sparks ideas for what you'd like to create.

Your Banner

Your banner is powerful because it gives us that first impression and feel for you/your work. I've always felt most comfortable creating a banner that has a picture of me looking right at the camera because

I'm a people person and I want my followers to get to know me. This is an inviting way to present yourself and it builds trust. You may want to use a different approach. Below I've shared a picture of my website banner.

Your Call to Action

It's important to have a way to get website visitors on your list. Remember that building your list is one of the most crucial aspects of the attract lever. It's what allows you to have a community of people who know, like, and trust you and who are interested in investing. It's a good idea to have a button on your banner where followers can join your list and get a great free offer in return. Here's a picture of my banner and free content offer below.

Your Home Page

A home page is powerful because its main job is to act as a business card. Your home page must quickly and clearly let people know who you are, who you work with, what problem you solve, and what desire you help your clients fulfill. Beyond that, everything else is just fluff or credibility features that you'll acquire as you continue growing your business and impact.

While I'll freely admit that I'm no pro website designer, my websites do a fantastic job of giving you the perfect feel for who I am and exactly what I do. My audience isn't confused about the offers that I present and it's why I can sell readings, development circles, and courses right off my site without a sales call or a high converting webinar.

While the home pages of long-term professional mediums may be pretty fancy with lots of impressive press icons, links to YouTube videos with 100s of 1000s or even millions of views, books, etc. don't sweat it if you just have a short simple page. I've told more than a few of my students over the years to simplify their home page by using fewer words that are more efficient at letting their audience know who they are and what they can help their ideal clients with.

Here are some great things to include on your home page:

- Banner *(optionally with a pic of you looking right at us)*
- Your Long Term Opt-In *(the free content you designed)*
- Your Name
- Navigation Bar *(so they can explore the rest of your site)*
- Some short and sweet words that clearly communicate the 3 Ps and direct them to become a subscriber

Your About Page

This is the time and place to tell a succinct and compelling version of your story. I don't mean to sound like an a-hole but not every part of our story is as interesting to other people as it is to ourselves. Think of your story as a timeline with different interesting events. When you list out all of the events, pick the ones that relate directly to your work and that give you credibility. You'll want to make sure that the details you include, and the way you tell your story exemplifies these six things below. Your story should:

- *Position you as an expert at what you do*
- *Make you relatable*
- *Show how likeable and interesting you are*
- *Display confidence*
- *Feel real and down to earth*
- *Include unique details that differentiate you from other people*

Once you've written your story on your about page, go through the list above and cross out each of the six things you've included. If you don't feel like you've achieved all of them, rework how you've written your story until you feel confident.

Your Services Page

It's important to have a place for your followers to go to learn about how they can work with you. Depending upon what your "just

starting" offers or "for the future" offers are, you might be able to simply have a description of your offers with a button to book. You can check this out on my services page using the QR code.

If one of your offers is a leveraged, medium to higher price point offer, then you'll want to create a sales page that inspires your lead to say yes. I'll be taking you through how to create a sales page, step-by-step in chapter nine. You can see in the picture below that if a client wants to look at my leveraged offers which are my courses or development circle, that there is a drop down on my navigation that brings viewers to the right place. Once they click, they are taken to the sales page of their choice.

When you're designing a services page or sales page, keep in mind that there should be no other calls to action. The only CTA on your services or sales page is a button to register for the service or program and become a paying client. You'll also want to make sure that there is no navigation bar. This is because once your followers are interested enough to browse your pages that give them an opportunity to invest in themselves through your work, you don't want them distracted by any other buttons that take them away from learning more about your offers.

Your Contact Page

Your contact page is there so that your followers have a way to get in touch with you and ask any question they might have. I've had people use the contact page to ask me when more reading appointments will be released, how to book a reading, if I'm interested in being interviewed, and much more. It's good to keep this page very simple. You can see an example of my contact page below.

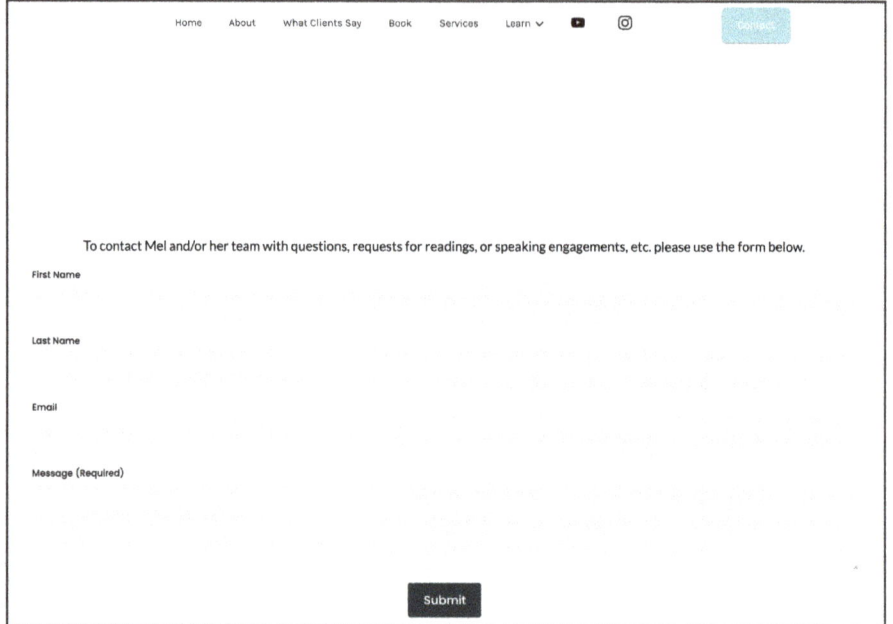

Your Testimonial Page

Testimonial pages are super straightforward too, yay! I have a picture on my page that says "What Clients Say" at the top of the page, similar to a simple banner. After that, I just add testimonial after testimonial as they come in. The thing about mediumship is that it's an industry that is well suited for referrals and word of mouth. When it comes to having someone bring through loved ones who have passed, everyone wants to make sure they're being referred to someone who is the real deal, and who is great at what they do. This is why a testimonials page is so important for you as a medium. I can already hear you panicking, "But I don't have any testimonials, I'm just starting!" That's ok. Take a deep breath and start asking everyone who sits with you if they're willing to answer a few questions after the reading. Here are the questions I ask my sitters post-reading.

- *How were you feeling before your reading with Mel? What were your expectations?*
- *How did you feel after your reading with Mel?*
- *Which parts of the reading or pieces of evidence stand out the most for you and what do they each mean for you? (Share as many as you can remember!)*
- *How would you describe your overall experience as a sitter during your reading with Mel?*
- *What would you say to anyone who is thinking of having an evidential mediumship reading with Mel?*

I put these questions in a google form and my clients' responses go into a google spreadsheet. I piece together their answers and edit them to make their responses flow as an overall statement. I send the statement to them over email, thanking them for sitting with me and asking permission in a no-pressure way to use it on my website. Some people ask me to use their first name only. This is a great way to create your testimonial page even before you start working professionally. I promise you that if you ask someone to write a testimonial for you without giving them prompts, you'll rarely get a response back. It's easier for them to say yes when you've done all of the work.

MAKING YOUR EXPOSURE TO POTENTIAL CLIENTS EXPERIENTIAL

Remember what we discussed in chapter four about displaying your work to the *right* people? Every person who follows you wants to know quickly what they'll get out of paying attention to you. They want fast and effective answers to their questions and solutions for their problems. The best thing you can do? *Show*, don't *tell*. I've said it before and I'll continue to say it throughout the rest of this book—you *must* create an *experience* for the leads who come across your work. We'll continue to discuss how to do this in the following chapters that focus on the nurture and invite parts of my Client Attraction Framework.

Think of your paid offers. You've also created free content, or at least have an idea for free content that will attract people who are interested in your offers. Now piece this together with the places that you've chosen to connect with people who are your ideal clients. How might you show up in a way that *displays* your work to these people? Does this start to give you an idea of how you might *show* the value of your work when you come into contact with people who would be the perfect fit as members of your ideal audience?

Remember that the offers I've chosen to focus on are my mediumship development circle and my course *Speaking With Spirits*. My free content features three easy exercises that my followers can use to strengthen their clair senses and speak to Spirit. You might notice just how congruent my free content is with my paid offers. The language matches too. Because I'll be using Instagram, YouTube, and a referral program, sharing how-to videos that display how I teach mediumship and recordings of many of the readings that I give to clients *shows* my prospects what it might be like to work with me. They don't have to use their imagination much or scroll through lots of written content to decide whether or not I resonate with them. Studies have shown that prospective clients spend an average of 2.9 seconds checking out your work before they decide if they're interested or not. That's *not* a lot of time. People have shorter attention spans today. They're not willing to do a lot of work to figure out the important details about you and your work. You have to do that work for them. Spend some time brainstorming what it might be like for you to display your work to the *right* people. You have enough of your business pieces in place. If you nail this part, I promise you that everything else I share will be easier, more fun, and a hell of a lot more effective as we continue on to the other parts of the Client Attraction Framework.

The most important thing for you to take away from this chapter is that learning to speak the language of your ideal client is the thing that will attract them. In everything you do and everything you share and create, use those 3 Ps like a champ. Make sure you're speaking to one specific person. Let them hear with your words that you understand their struggles and that you have the ability to help them get the result, or have the experience, that they want.

CHAPTER 7

NURTURE

CREATING CONNECTION AND A GENUINE RELATIONSHIP WITH YOUR SPIRITUAL COMMUNITY

You're spending time in the nurture category when you're doing any work in your business that helps you hone your ability to inspire connection in your community, build genuine relationships, and serve with integrity. Anything you do that allows a follower to get to know you, like you, and truly trust you falls under the nurture part of the Client Attraction Framework. This is a precious use of your time and most definitely considered a client-getting action. You must create relationships with the people you're looking to work with just as you would a dear friend. As you work through this chapter, you'll notice that there are a lot of references to the invitation aspect of the Client Attraction Framework. This is because the nurture and invite parts of the framework overlap a lot. You can't really have one without the other.

When it comes to approaching your ideal clients online or in person, please oh please, put the relationship first! Don't be a douche by coming across as a used car salesman. "Hey, got any money? Want to buy something?" I know it's unlikely you had that pick-up line in mind, but what I'm saying is that you must focus on *first* connecting, and *then* making the appropriate invitation at the appropriate time. Premature marriage proposals aren't hot. How often do you witness offers, especially online, that feel like too much too soon from people you've never met or barely know? My biggest pet peeve is when I get emails from people I've never met offering to "help me with my website" by giving me an unsolicited critique. I don't usually take the time to respond and say, "No thank you, asshat." Then there are the DMs I get on Instagram offering to help me grow my online marketing business from my account that I haven't posted on for over four years. A little bit of research and more effort to build a relationship with me would have gone a long way.

Do you ever feel afraid of coming off the same way? Do you feel like you're simultaneously battling that voice inside your head that's saying, *I really want clients! What can I do or say to get clients ASAP?*

We've all had our awkward moments reaching out to ideal prospects. I hesitate to tell you this story, but there was a time when I reached my climax of shameful moments as a business owner. Early in my career, I was reading a book that encouraged striking up conversations with new people. The idea was that these conversations would lead to new clients. I preface this story with the excuse that I was 25, desperate, and broke when it happened.

Here's how it actually played out. Believe it or not, I creepily wandered the aisles of a Barnes and Noble bookstore in Greenwich Village in NYC with the goal of meeting new prospective clients. I did have conversations, but they were with random strangers. They were also the most cringeworthy conversations of my life. What started as a natural hello and continued on to chit chat that displayed our shared love of books was quickly followed up by a non sequitur that made a shameful beeline for my business. These people were clearly becoming more and more cautious by the moment. I ended the conversations by asking for their email so I could add them to my marketing list. Most people looked agonizingly uncomfortable as they said no and quickly walked away from me. Others left via speed walking and there were two or three who ran. The few who said yes never responded to any of my follow up emails. Surprise, surprise!

If you set the intention to genuinely connect with someone *first*, it's unlikely you'll have a story to tell that's as ridiculous and embarrassing as the one I just shared. Suffice it to say that it's worth putting in the time and effort to learn to be curious about others and treat them like humans instead of numbers.

Here's another story that will help you understand the biggest mistakes most of us make in our approach to allowing followers to become paid clients. It was April of 2018, and my mom was being inaugurated as the president of a women's college in Milwaukee, Wisconsin. Our immediate family and much of our extended family came to celebrate. My parents invited all of their friends. Ken was one of those friends.

Ken was a nice guy with a big heart and a deep desire to connect with others. Unfortunately, within 48 hours, and well before the long weekend was over, every single person at the get-together was avoiding Ken like the plague. I felt guilty and confused for wanting to avoid Ken myself. He was a kind, well-intentioned person. Why was this happening?

At the end of the day, Rob and I were chatting before bed and discussing the Ken situation. I realized the crux of the problem was twofold. First, Ken was looking to experience all of the benefits of a close personal relationship, but without putting in the time to build a foundation of trust. His attempts to connect felt like an overstepping of boundaries because they demanded too much, too soon.

Second, interactions with Ken weren't really interactions at all. They were one-sided *presentations* that didn't invite much, if any, participation. I thought about my experience with Ken over the past 48 hours. Ken rarely asked questions of others, except for the occasional deep, and somewhat invasive, personal questions that he'd ask abruptly. Within moments, you'd realize that they were used to strategically circle back to a story of his own that he desperately wanted to tell, before you could answer. Ken enthusiastically hijacked any conversation. He held you captive with long stories about his personal life journey. In a matter of minutes, and before you'd spent any significant amount of time with him, it was easy to feel like connecting with Ken was asking a lot more of you than perhaps you felt comfortable giving.

As I reflect on the story of Ken, I realize just how easy it is as well-meaning, passionate, mission driven entrepreneurs to unknowingly demand too much too soon from those we see as our ideal potential clients. You may be able to draw parallels between the story of Ken, and your experience with marketing both as a business owner and when you're on the receiving end. My intention behind sharing the story of Ken is not to dissuade you from confidently making invitations to your audience. Instead, it's a powerful reminder that we must learn to create interactive experiences with our ideal clients rather than one-sided presentations. We must create know, like, and trust that merits the level of commitment that we're asking for when extending invitations to our audience.

When I tell you to nurture your audience, think about a relationship you have with a good friend. How do you nurture that relationship? You reach out often. You chat with them pretty consistently, right? Of course that's a simplistic way of looking at it, but for now, that's the bird's eye view of what it means to nurture your audience.

I'm excited to share three elements that majorly encourage trust. These elements will help you create more of an experience for your ideal clients. They are my recipe for accelerated audience attraction and next-level nurturing in the online world. When you become masterful at using them, they inspire your audience to say yes to your invitations more often.

Have you ever noticed how some people seem to easily create powerful online and/or in-person engagement while others struggle to get noticed? Let's crack the code on why this happens so that you can create lasting connections with the people you serve. We need to be able to understand what compels our ideal audience to want to spend time with us online in order to make an impact and invite those who need our support into our profitable client pathway.

I've spent years studying these elements. I've conducted my research in the online and in-person marketing space. I've asked people over and over again what inspires them to engage and creates those feelings of knowing, liking, and trusting the experts they follow. Here are the three crucial elements that I've found matter the most.

1) Expertise

The Expertise element is your ability to provide value and show yourself as the expert you are. There are many ways to include the element of expertise when you market your business:

- Sharing content/info that's needed to fulfil their P for pleasure
- Teaching/methods/frameworks that lead to "ah-has" and are communicated in a compelling and memorable way
- Being able to help solve the problems of your target market and quickly
- Displaying depth of knowledge and confidence in that knowledge
- Ability to extract a higher performance from your target market than they can on their own without your help
- Credibility elements (certifications, experience, etc.)

Be generous with your followers when you share information and content to help solve their pain points. To create more trust, think about unique ways that you can allow them to experience your work and get a quick result. Perhaps a step-by-step in a how-to video that enables them to create a fast win. You can intentionally include the expertise element each time you connect with your audience. Brainstorm some ideas.

2) Resonance

The resonance element is your ability to create feelings of alignment and connection with your target audience. There are many ways to include the element of resonance when you market your business:

- Sharing your mission
- Using the power of story
- Behind the scenes views of what you teach and how you walk your talk
- Being yourself and committing to being relatable, honest, and sometimes vulnerable
- Social proof, client case studies, and testimonials
- Demonstrating a genuine belief in and care for your clients

The resonance element is all about knowing your own values and beliefs and being able to share them effectively to the people you want to work with. Business owners who create strong resonance with their ideal audience pay attention to how their ideal clients' respond. They notice what resonates on a deep level with their people. The resonance element is just one reason that research is so important. As you get to know your followers, you'll more clearly understand what they resonate with. Think about ways you can use elements of resonance, like story substance and client testimonials, to allow those who follow you to experience an emotional shift or deep connection with you. Their time with you will feel more like an interactive experience as you master this. How can you intentionally include the resonance element each time you connect with your audience? Brainstorm some ideas.

3) Engagement

The engagement element is about creating opportunities to interact and engage with your audience. We'll be revisiting this element in our next chapter and going deeper. For now, there are many ways to include the element of engagement when you market your business:

- Asking your target market to open/read, respond, comment or reply to an email/blog
- Inviting your target market to comment or interact with you on live video
- Inviting your target mark to follow you online in different places or join your list
- Asking your target market to answer questions during a live event (i.e. speaking event, webinar, etc.)
- Q&A opportunities of any kind
- Any opportunity for your target market to respond to a CTA

The engagement element is all about inviting your audience to spend time with you. Look to *continually* make small, generally free, and easy to say yes to invitations to your audience. What are simple questions you can ask or engagement prompts you can include that your audience can respond to and that can create more of an interactive experience for them? Think about how you can intentionally include the engagement element each time you look to market to and connect with your audience. Brainstorm some ideas.

Take a look at this **Next Level Nurturing** diagram below. This diagram illustrates the power of masterfully incorporating all three elements each time you interact with your audience and share about your work.

This killer combo helps you to create know, like, and trust and build an experience for your leads. Landing in the Exceptional Zone is the key to attracting a following online and nurturing that following in a powerful way that leads to conversions, regardless of the online platform or client attraction strategy.

There is no limit to *how* you might include all three of these elements. Each time you craft an email, social post, notes for a live or recorded video, etc., use these three elements as a checklist to make sure you're not leaving any of them out. It's easy to only use one or two. Unfortunately, that lands you outside of the Exceptional Zone. Few business owners take the time to become masterful at all three.

NEXT LEVEL NURTURING

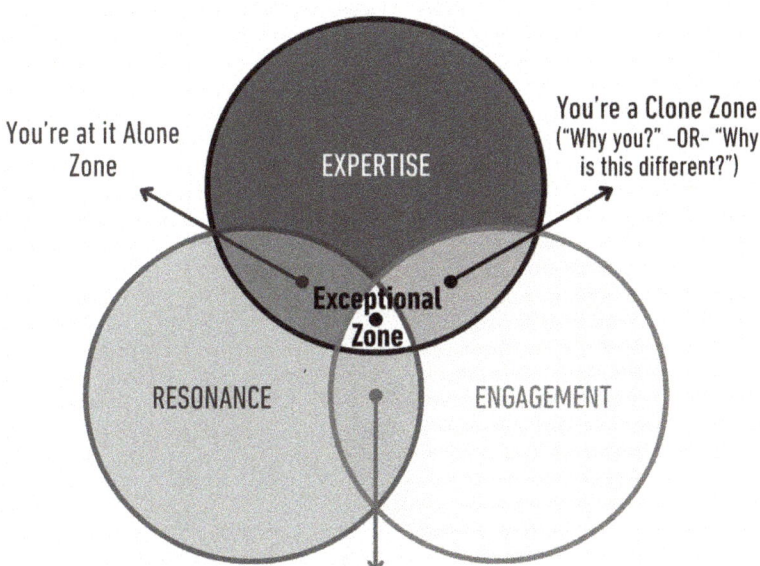

You're at it Alone Zone

EXPERTISE

You're a Clone Zone ("Why you?" -OR- "Why is this different?")

Exceptional Zone

RESONANCE

ENGAGEMENT

Throw Me a Bone Zone ("That's so nice" Department)

- If you're great at providing expertise and resonance, but you're not getting engagement, you're at it alone. As engagement grows, sales grow. People don't want to be told things. They want to have an experience. At the very least, they want to feel that your expertise is something they can implement for themselves and that what you have to offer will work for them.
- If you're providing resonance and engagement, but the expertise just isn't there, then you gotta throw your peeps a bone! They're here to learn from an expert so do your thing and don't hold back.
- If you're providing expertise and engagement, but you're not resonating with your audience, you might as well be a clone of someone else teaching the same thing. When it comes time to make their choice about where to invest, they'll choose someone else that they resonate with more.

Be creative as you combine these three elements. Always intentionally create more of an interactive experience for your audience than a one-sided presentation. For example, I constantly had followers asking me the best ways to strengthen their skills as a medium. I decided to create a YouTube video and I named it *The top 4 things I did to strengthen my skills as a medium.* In it, I showcased my expertise by sharing how I gave 100 free readings to begin my journey to becoming a professional medium. I also shared my knowledge of Sitting in the Power—a great practice for mediums. All of the content I included displayed that I had a lot of knowledge about mediumship and the mechanics of how it all works. To create resonance with my audience, I shared behind-the-scenes moments on my journey, like feeling nervous before readings and going through mediumship development cycles where my readings were inconsistent. In my video, I ask them what they feel has helped them strengthen their skills the most. I also give them easy yes invitations at the end like commenting on my video, liking it, or sharing. I even share my free content to invite them onto my list. All of these invitations invite them to engage with me in different ways that are 100% appropriate for the high-quality content that I generously share during the video. The videos create an experience for them that gives them the feel of what it's like to be in a class of mine. This makes it easier for them to imagine investing in themselves through my development circle or course.

Below is a step-by-step example of how I might reverse engineer nurturing my audience in a way that includes all three elements.

HOW TO REVERSE ENGINEER NURTURING YOUR AUDIENCE

Even before I include these three elements, I make a decision about what the *purpose* of connecting with my audience is. It might be as simple as building trust. Perhaps your purpose is to convert yeses to an invitation of yours from any of the three levels of your Client Pathway Pyramid. Either way, don't forget to keep the invitation appropriate in terms of the environment and trust level.

1) What's the purpose of this nurturing client-getting action?

The purpose will be to grow my subscriber list with ideal clients leading up to the launch of my mediumship course *Speaking With Spirits*. Decide upon a client-getting nurture action for yourself and what the purpose of it is.

EXPERTISE

2) What's the #1 top of mind desire that your ideal audience member has?

The best way to answer this question is to think about their top P for pleasure. What is the number one result they care about the most? You might think about the FAQs you get most often. You can also go about it from a different angle and think about the fire that they need putting out most. In other words, what is their biggest obstacle when it comes to achieving their greatest desire? My ideal client's greatest desires or pleasure points might be one of the examples I've shared below.

- *Feel more confident as a medium*
- *Give mind-blowing readings with jaw-dropping evidence*
- *Become a good enough medium to get paid for readings*

3) What step or tool from your framework can help them get that result?

It's helpful to think about what you could teach them that will help them with their topmost struggle or the thing they want most. It's vital to make sure that they are conscious of the struggle or greatest desire they have. If they don't realize it's a desire or struggle for them, then your attempt to nurture your relationship with them won't be compelling enough. Think about what steps or tools you teach that might be the most exciting for them, as well as effective. I've shared an example below of how each of those top desires I listed above has a corresponding tool alongside it.

- *Feel more confident as a medium*
- *Tool: Mediumship Affirmations Meditation for Confidence*
- *Give mind-blowing readings with jaw-dropping evidence*

- *Tool: A combination of clair strengthening exercises*
- *Become a good enough medium to get paid for readings*
- *Tool: My special training How to Give Your BEST Mediumistic Reading*

After you've listed tools to accompany the top desires for your ideal clients, choose the one that you think is most compelling for your followers. For me, the second or third options are definitely the sexiest ones. As you know, I've created my free content around clair strengthening exercises so this will be the tool that I choose because I know for certain that it's a juicy topic for my ideal clients.

4) What's your favorite way to share your expertise?

In chapter six you decided upon your attraction platform(s). Your choice(s) will likely give you ideas for the best way to share your expertise in an effort to nurture your audience. For me, I'd likely create both a recorded YouTube video and a live video on Instagram. What might be a way for you to connect with your people in a way that suits you? Here are some ideas below.

- Live or recorded video content
- Written content like a published article, blog post, social post, or email
- Speaking

RESONANCE

It's time to choose one of your top stories or story snippets that will resonate deeply with your audience. Story is the easiest way to connect with others and find common ground, and it should be easy for them to see themselves in the story you share. It's a chance to illustrate the value of spending their time with you and to discover that they align with who you are. Plus, it's often the reason they choose you over someone else who could technically teach them the same thing. I love to share one of two stories that resonate with my audience. One is the story of what I call my "holy shit" reading. It was one of the first readings that I ever gave and it was full of jaw-dropping evidence. I used all of my clairs and I was able to give a highly accurate reading. The other is a story snippet about a client who, after a class of mine, gave a fantastic reading using the exact strategies that I teach to help my clients strengthen their clairs. What stories or story snippets come to mind for you?

ENGAGEMENT

We'll be diving more deeply into how to create engagement in the chapter ten lessons that focus on the invite step of my Client Attraction Framework. For now, get in the habit of always giving your audience an opportunity to interact with you. When you create opportunities to engage with you, it may lead to your followers deciding to join your list, becoming a more committed member of your audience, or even investing with you. The main goal is to create continuous engagement and interaction that creates connection, a relationship, and an experiential feel. Below I've listed some simple examples of invitations that are easy to say yes to.

- Follow you on a social media platform
- Like or comment on your written or video social media post
- Join your online community by opting in for free content
- Share your content or pass along a good word about you to a friend or family member
- Register for a webinar or event you're hosting

- Invite them continuously to interact, answer questions, or comment in response to anything you share about your work

My YouTube videos share compelling content that leads viewers to my opt-in about strengthening their clairs, but I share more than just a single invitation per YouTube video. For example, during a video, I might ask a question that relates to the video topic like, "Let me know what your dominant clair or clairs are." This is a question that I know my people love to answer. I could also ask, "Share what clair you want to strengthen most" or "What is the best piece of evidence you've brought through during a reading? What clair did you use to receive the evidence?" Another way to engage your audience is to ask them to vote on which clair they want you to share some free content about next and then you could respond in real time by sharing that information or some helpful tidbits.

Once you've thought through your answers to the questions in this chapter and planned how you can include the three elements, I suggest creating a practice social post or live video or an email to your list or referral network to nurture your audience so that you can get on your way to becoming masterful at landing in the Zone of Excellence. You'll see from the diagram that landing in the Zone of Excellence happens when you nurture your audience using all three elements.

- Expertise *(The 3 Ps should be obvious and convey the value)*
- Resonance *(Time for your story substance element to shine)*
- Engagement *(How can you invite them to interact and engage with you)*

HOW OFTEN TO NURTURE YOUR AUDIENCE

At this point the question I always get is, "Mel, how often should I nurture my audience?" In chapter six you identified your attraction platforms aka the places that your ideal clients hang out where you can connect with them. Bring those to mind now.

You'll remember that my three ways or places to connect with my ideal clients are YouTube, Instagram, and through my referral system. These people for the most part are on my email list. A percentage of your followers from every place you go to connect should ideally be ending up on your list by subscribing to your free content. Below, I've created a calendar that shows how often I nurture my audience—at a minimum—via each of my attraction platforms and my list.

	Monday	Tuesday	Wed	Thurs	Friday	Saturday	Sunday
Email List				1/wk min			
YouTube				1/wk			
Instagram		2/wk		2/wk			
Referral Network		1/mo or quarter					

No matter what attraction platform(s) you've chosen, you should have a nurture schedule that includes emailing your list of subscribers that you'll be growing via your free content that your ideal leads can opt in for on your attraction platforms.

You'll notice that I email my list of subscribers at least once a week. I can't tell you how often I talk to entrepreneurs who haven't emailed their list for weeks or months or who don't email their subscribers consistently. This is a way of squandering one of your most precious resources. It takes work, time, and patience to grow a list of subscribers, so if you do nothing else, take good care of them. Remember to think of them as dear friends who you show up for constantly. I am extremely consistent with my subscribers and I email them every Thursday with my latest published YouTube video and any other important content and information that I'd like to share.

I remember a student saying to me, "I love watching your YouTube videos so much! Can you send us an email when you release your videos?" Another student instantly jumped in before I could respond and said, "She sends an email every Thursday when she releases her newest YouTube video to let you know it's out, but you have to subscribe to her list." For me, as nerdy as this sounds, it was a moment of triumph! I love it when I see signs of my constant, high-quality nurturing paying off.

You'll see in the calendar that I nurture my audience once a week on YouTube. I do this by releasing my latest how-to video or recorded reading, etc. It's nice because it actually serves as no-brainer content for my weekly email.

For Instagram, I engage much less than the average bear. You'll remember me saying that social media is not my favorite place to be, right? My own personal promise to myself when I began my IG account for my mediumship business was that I would never require myself to create content and be active more than two times a week. An IG expert might call this sacrilege, but ask me how many effs I give? For me, it works well enough because my other attraction platforms are highly efficient so my IG account is one more place to follow me and back up the credibility I've created in other places.

You'll see that I connect with my referral network about once a quarter. How do I do this? When I have a client or even a non-client who refers other clients to me, I put their name on my referral network list. Most of the time, when I'm reaching out to my referral network, it's just to touch base and say hello like you would to a good friend. Every six months or so, I let them know what I've been up to lately and the main ways that I'm supporting clients. I might also let them in on free services, bonuses, or prizes they might be eligible for when they refer clients to me if I'm in the middle of a launch for my development circle or a course. For every offer that someone invests in, they have to fill out a form and answer the question, "How did you hear about Mel?" This is how I keep track of what percentage of my clientele comes from each of my attraction platforms.

The example I shared on my previous calendar is pretty miniscule. One of the reasons I can get away with being online so little and reaching out to my list once a week, and my referral network once a quarter, is because my video content on YouTube is being seen by followers and new prospects 24x7. There are no hard and fast rules about quantity, although social media experts may disagree. The thing that I find to be the most important is the quality of the nurturing that you do—this means *always* including EER—and the consistency. With consistency, I'll add that communicating with your audience less than once a week just isn't enough. We live in a fast-paced world and you'll need to be top of mind to be the first person your ideal clients reach out to when they need the help you provide.

I've shared another calendar below, showcasing what a typical nurture week looks like when I'm more active and launching a course or development circle.

	Monday	Tuesday	Wed	Thurs	Friday	Saturday	Sunday
Email List		X	X	X	X		
YouTube				X			
Instagram		X	X	X			
Referral Network		1/every 2 weeks					

Create your own schedule and do what feels right to you, but that has you engaging no less often than my initial calendar. Even if a social media platform is an attraction platform for you, while you may need to be active more often than I am, know that a single high-quality post – like a video that lands in the Zone of Excellence – could be the thing that gets your business a lot of attention. It doesn't take the place of being consistent and showing up over and over again, but the quality of your interactions will always be more important than constantly being on a platform and posting a zillion times a day.

REPURPOSING CONTENT FOR CONSISTENCY

One of the things that can keep us from consistently connecting with our audience is not knowing what to talk about. Maybe you've wondered how to create enough valuable content to continuously feel like you have something compelling to say. To solve the first problem, I'll simply point you to your framework(s) that you designed in chapter five. You can look at your steps and tools to get an idea of what you might share that is a must have topic for your audience.

I used to worry that if I wrote about a certain topic I had to cross it off my list and not use it again for a long time. The thing I had to remind myself was that my followers are a few steps behind me. That means they benefit greatly from hearing the same information many times and actually require repetition in order to develop new skills and transform.

To switch it up, it's less about finding new topics, steps, or tools, and more about:

- developing many different ways to say the same thing as you share and display your expertise

- creatively incorporating unique stories and elements of resonance
- using different calls to action and invitations to engage

Once you have a CRF/CEF and you truly understand your ideal client, you can be creative in terms of repurposing your content. This allows you to be visible and build trust while also being seen as the go-to expert for your audience. Below is my step-by-step system for repurposing content.

1) Notice what's top of mind for your audience.

Reference your CRF/CEF and choose something that matches up with the topics that are most important to your audience. For example, if a follower is saying they have such a hard time hearing clairaudiently, create some powerful content that features effective exercises for strengthening clairaudience. Add at least one Free Easy Yes invitation! Bam.

What are the main struggles your ideal clients are mentioning or asking you about? If you don't know, remember to check out the online discussions of your ideal clients on another medium's social account, blog, etc. You can also think about your own struggles that you've overcome and know are common for your ideal client.

2) Divide your theme/topic into smaller (bite-sized) pieces.

Create subject lines for these smaller topics that you can send to your email list. They could also be the title of live video reels that you post on a social media platform. It could be the subject line of a personal email that you send to some of your most powerful referral partners, telling them what you've been noticing lately with your ideal clients. If you're a blogger, you could use them for blog content. I divide my topics multiple times to get bite-sized content, and to create many different opportunities to share my expertise. This also works because you're not giving away the store. You're giving them a small piece of what you dive deeply into in your paid services or products.

> Ex) My overall theme/topic is Developing Your Clairaudience for Better Spirit Communication.

I've divided that theme/topic into three smaller pieces of content that showcase my expertise and help put out the huge clairaudient bonfire that I've noticed my audience has.

> Email #1 = My favorite exercise(s) to develop clairaudience
>
> Email #2 = How to get better at hearing names clairaudiently
>
> Email #3 = Easy ways to develop clairaudience that don't take much time

As you look at the examples I created, think about what smaller content topics you can create from your theme. Make sure to create at least three.

3) Repurpose your three mini-content topics.

Depending on how you chose to share your first mini topic, repurpose it in another way. If you shared it as an email, now share the same content as a video reel on a social platform. If you shared it as a video, send it out to your list as an email. If you shared it in both of those ways initially, send it out as an update to your referral partners so they know what you're up to. Invite them to pass it along to someone else they think might appreciate your expertise.

Ex) From the email/blog topics that I created above, I've developed titles that I can use for live video and for the subject lines of my emails and blog posts. You can always reference chapter six for help creating compelling titles.

Live Video Title #1 = My favorite exercise to develop clairaudience

Live Video Title #2 = How to get better at hearing names clairaudiently

Live Video Title #3 = The #1 easiest way to become clairaudient

Live Video Title #4 = How music can help you become more clairaudient

Live Video Title #5 = A behind the scenes share of the clairaudient symbols I use with Spirit

How might you repurpose your content? Where could you share it on one additional attraction platform where your ideal clients hang out? Create 3-5 titles below and don't be afraid to reuse some of the same titles that you've used elsewhere.

All of the expertise that I share when I connect with my ideal clients comes from a pre-determined weekly theme. Yes, I use the process I just walked you through. My YouTube content becomes my email content, which then becomes my IG content, which then becomes something I bring up when I interact with clients in any other place. There's no reinventing the wheel. If I want to, I'll create a theme for the whole month so that I don't feel like I have to go through this process on a weekly basis. Once I create my overall theme/topic I'm not creating anything else new to showcase my expertise. What are your ideas about how you'll repurpose your content online?

CHAPTER 8

INVITE

CREATING INVITATIONS THAT TURN PROSPECTS INTO PAYING CUSTOMERS

You're spending time in the invite category when you're doing any work in your business that invites your followers to engage with you. Anything you do that allows a follower to respond to an invitation to engage and therefore enables them to truly get to know you, like you, and trust you falls under this aspect of the Client Attraction Framework. I can't tell you how often I see entrepreneurs shy away from making invitations to their audience—even small ones. It's a shame because this is a crucially important use of your time and is most definitely considered a client-getting action! The more you make invitations that are easy and fun to say yes to, the more you show your audience that spending time with you leaves them off better than they were before. They'll begin to see that you can be trusted to help solve their biggest pain points and to help them achieve their greatest pleasure points too.

USING INVITATIONS AS YOUR GREATEST OPPORTUNITY FOR ONLINE CONVERSIONS

The upcoming diagrams in this chapter are two different illustrations of how you might view and organize offers along your Client Pathway Pyramid. This should look familiar since we took our first look at the CPP in chapter four when we discussed creating a business model that provides a pathway to profitability.

Wahoo, you have your *just starting* offer(s) decided upon at this point and they are likely low, medium, or high price point offers that require some moola being forked over. Don't forget that Free Easy Yes offers are just as important even though they don't require a financial investment.

In fact, Free Easy Yes offers are where we'll be primarily focusing when we pull the invite lever of the Client Attraction Framework. I can't emphasize enough just how powerful it is to create free opportunities for your audience to interact with you.

I remember when I was a personal trainer long ago at the age of 23 when I'd just moved to Boston. I'd walk around the gym socializing with the members, offering a hand anywhere I could. I was happy to answer questions and display my expertise when people needed suggestions or advice. If it felt right, I'd kindly ask permission to share a generous tip that was above and beyond the expectations of our gym members. You bet it wasn't long before these people started coming to me for training.

Free Easy Yes invitations help you build trust, prioritize relationships, and create an experience with your clients that keeps you top of mind. Each time you make a Free Easy Yes invitation, you create an opportunity to deliver value and show your people that good things happen when they say yes to spending time with you.

I've circled Free Easy Yes invitations on both diagrams as the "Greatest Opportunity for Online Conversions." That's because this first level of the Client Pathway Pyramid is fertile ground for two things. First, building a relationship with leads by extending Free Easy Yes invitations that overdeliver. Second, creating onramps to your Client Pathway Pyramid that eventually lead to your paid offers.

The common mistake is to use whatever attraction platforms you've identified for mostly paid invitations without creating an appropriate level of know, like, and trust *first* via Free Easy Yes invitations.

The key is to become masterful at consistently making Free Easy Yes invitations that create trust and the opportunity for leads to enter your Client Pathway Pyramid. Think of it this way: before you propose marriage, you've hopefully gone out for lots of coffees, walks, dinners, movie nights, etc. Popping the question is the paid offer, and all of these dates are the Free Easy Yes invitations. Of course there are times when making low, medium, and high price point invitations is appropriate, but remember: Build trust and a relationship first.

An example of this might be creating a live video where you share juicy drool-worthy content that incorporates all three E, E, and R elements. People feel blown away by your generosity and the quality of your free content. In this case, it might not feel premature to offer a paid service or product at the end of the video. It is important though, to make sure that your audience has had enough time to trust you by experiencing plenty of Free Easy Yes invitations. Sometimes you can get to a paid offer sooner if trust has been transferred to them via a referral source. You can think of this as a date that is set up for you by someone you know and trust already, who tells you this person is a perfect match for you.

Either way, it's about the trust in their relationship with you, matching the level of the invitation that you're making. This is the most direct path to earning paid clients. You wouldn't make a marriage proposal during your first coffee date with someone. So, it makes sense that you won't get far desperately throwing out low, medium, and high price point offers before your followers have much of a chance to get to know you.

Set an intention to do next level nurturing that creates meaningful connections and that invites ideal leads into your pathway with integrity. Continue using the elements of E, E, and R to nurture your leads and convert them to higher level offers!

Take a look at both of the diagrams below. In a notebook, fill in each level with your current offers. Once you've done that, focus mainly on filling that first level with as many ideas for Free Easy Yes invitations that you can think of. This exercise will get your mind thinking creatively about how you can prioritize building trust and creating powerful experiences for your audience.

CLIENT PATHWAY PYRAMID

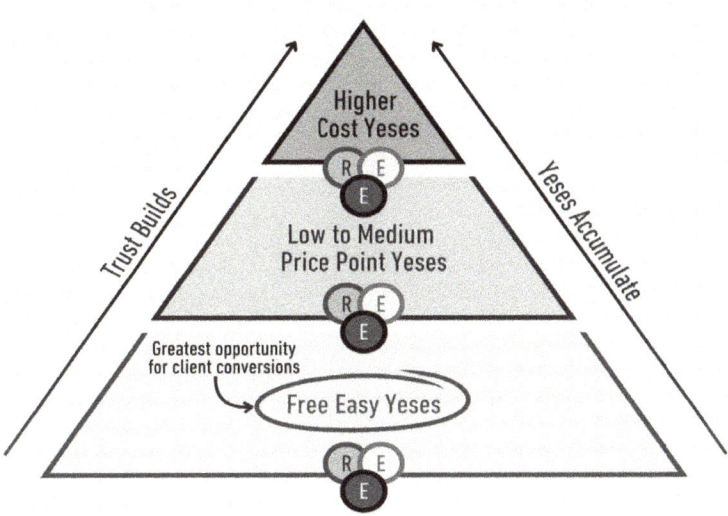

CLIENT PATHWAY PYRAMID

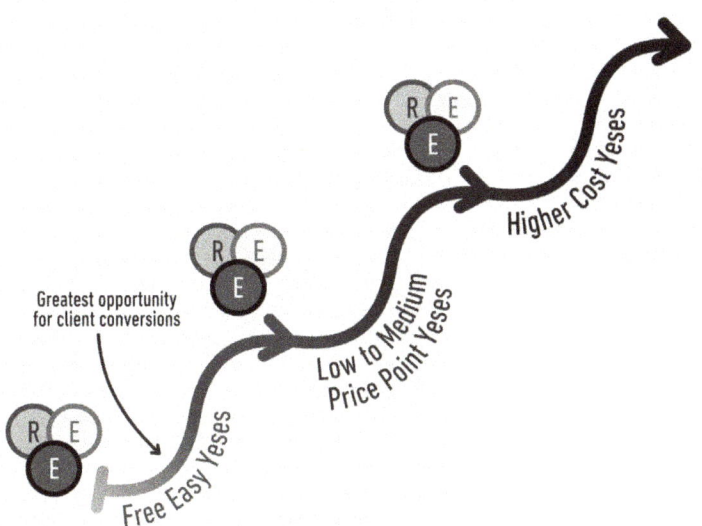

As we focus on your greatest opportunity for conversions in the Free Easy Yes level of the pyramid, I'm sharing the version of the CPP once more that focuses on examples of those kinds of offers.

CLIENT PATHWAY PYRAMID

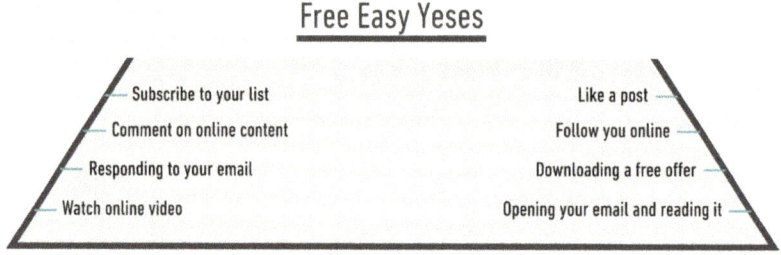

I've listed different types of Free Easy Yeses below.

- Watch an online video
- Like an online post
- Comment on online content
- Follow you online
- Check out your website
- Private message you online or send you an email
- Download a free offer
- Subscribe to your list

- Open your email
- Respond to an email
- Click on a link in your email

This is not an exhaustive list by any means. What I want you to note, is that a lot of these Free Easy Yeses don't even require you to make an actual invitation to someone. If you're nurturing your audience like we discussed in chapter seven, then potential prospects will naturally become curious. They'll start taking actions like following you online, opting in as a subscriber, checking out your website, and beginning to comment on your free content. Yes, all of these examples are free, easy to do, and a way for your followers to say yes to engaging with you whether you've asked them to do these things or not.

While it can be appropriate to make paid invitations from your attraction platforms, I want you to understand that Free Easy Yeses are exactly as they sound. They are super easy opportunities for your ideal prospects to start engaging without feeling pushed or obligated. If you know anything about healthy relationships, you know that relationships where there is space for someone to build trust in a way that feels safe and comfortable for them are the ones that last. They are quality relationships. They are the kind of relationships you want with your audience members if you want a financially sustainable business that is also fulfilling and meaningful to you and your clients.

THE CLIENT ATTRACTION LEVERS TO PULL ON A DAILY AND WEEKLY BASIS!

I'd like you to think about the 5-Part Client Attraction Framework, specifically parts two, three, and four. We'll dive deeper into those skills in the upcoming chapters and lessons. In order to get to the point where ideal prospects are showing interest and reaching out, you need to be working parts two, (attract) three, (nurture) and four (invite) each time you market your business via your attraction platforms.

Below, I've shown an example of a weekly marketing calendar. I've outlined details about my attempt to connect in a way that shares how I use each interaction to attract, nurture, and invite my audience on a daily and weekly basis. I'm very purposeful when I market my business. I always know the ultimate reason I'm attempting to connect. I make a habit of asking myself two questions beforehand.

1) What is your overarching goal for your business in the next 90 days?

What would you like to see happen in your mediumship business in the next 90 days? Use the 5-part framework to help you stay focused. For example, in terms of clarity, what offer will you be marketing? How many new clients would you like? You should know who you'll be marketing it to and the price point. For me, I'll say that it's my mediumship course, *Speaking With Spirits.* Let's say that I'd like 50 students to enroll in my course at my $997 price point. Next, think about part two, attract. How many new subscribers would you like to attract? In my second year of business, I attracted about 120 YouTube followers a month and about 25-30 subscribers to my list. Third is nurture. How would you like to nurture your audience on a regular basis? I know YouTube videos are my primary way. We've just discussed how to invite your audience to engage. With these parts of the framework in mind, what is your overarching goal for the next 90 days? For me, I'll say it's to enroll 50 people in my course, *Speaking With Spirits,* to attract 100 more subscribers on my list and 400 more subscribers to my YouTube channel.

2) What actions will you need to take on a daily and weekly basis to accomplish your 90 day goal?

Clarity

Ex. 1) I'll need to make sure my audience is aware of my course. I'll do this by sharing more details about it and the upcoming enrollment without actually making the offer yet.

Attract

Ex. 2) I'll need to make sure there are plenty of ways for those who come across me to opt in via my free content as a subscriber on my list so I can grow my audience leading up to enrollment.

Nurture

Ex. 3) I'll need to make sure I'm consistently nurturing my audience and even amp up how often I nurture them. I'll do this with YouTube videos, some IG videos, and emails to my list.

Invite

Ex. 4) I need to make sure that each time I nurture my audience, I give them an opportunity to engage with me and have a positive experience with my work. This is why I always ask people to comment on my videos and I send out emails asking my subscribers for feedback.

All of your actions should tie together so your efforts are leading in the same direction to your 90 day goal. This will be more efficient and help you to create positive momentum.

Check out this calendar that I've shared below. It shows you how I pull the levers of attract, nurture, and invite on a weekly and daily basis to get the marketing wheels of my business turning. I've added a row at the bottom of the table that acts as a checklist for E, E, and R. This will make it more likely that your marketing will be high quality and land in the Zone of Excellence.

At this point, you've done *most* of the crucial work that will have the kind of people you want to work with walking through your door. You've got clarity about who you want to work with. You know what you're offering to help them overcome their pain points and reach their pleasure points. You know the price point(s) of your offer(s). You've learned how important it is to attract, nurture, and invite your audience to engage with you.

It's time for you to design your own calendar that helps you make sure that you're pulling the three levers of attract, nurture, and invite on a daily and weekly basis. This will show your potential clients how you can help them and the opportunities that are available to them.

Monday	Tuesday	Wednesday	Thursday	Friday
PURPOSE: Start spreading the word about my course *Speaking With Spirits*, grow my list by 100 subscribers, and nurture my followers so they are ready to invest when enrollment opens.	**PURPOSE:** Start spreading the word about my course *Speaking With Spirits*, grow my list by 100 subscribers, and nurture my followers so they are ready to invest when enrollment opens.	**PURPOSE:** Start spreading the word about my course *Speaking With Spirits*, grow my list by 100 subscribers, and nurture my followers so they are ready to invest when enrollment opens.	**PURPOSE:** Start spreading the word about my course *Speaking With Spirits*, grow my list by 100 subscribers, and nurture my followers so they are ready to invest when enrollment opens.	**PURPOSE:** Start spreading the word about my course *Speaking With Spirits*, grow my list by 100 subscribers, and nurture my followers so they are ready to invest when enrollment opens.
CLIENT GETTING ACTION: Behind The Scenes IG Reel sharing **something I learned in a reading.** I'll share simple step-by-step content that puts out the fire of my ideal client. It'll be how to get better at identifying the spirit quickly and accurately. *(A)(N)* During my reel I'll ask questions after each tip that I share. I'll also ask them to share their biggest takeaway at the end. I'll let them know I have some free content about strengthening their clairs to opt in for and share the URL. *(I)(A)*	**CLIENT GETTING ACTION:** IG Live content that is also **repurposed as an email to my list** that intersects with the support I provide and the needs of my ideal client. It can be on the topic of confidence as a medium. *(A)(N)* I'll let them know the four main ways I'll be helping my students improve their confidence in my new course with an invitation to join the waitlist before enrollment opens. *(I)*	**CLIENT GETTING ACTION:** 30 minutes engaging with my **leads via email/IG/YouTube.** I'll thoughtfully answer any questions I receive via email, YT, or IG. *(N)* I'll share a resource with them like my opt in or a YouTube video that helps and also let them know I'm going deeper in my upcoming course *Speaking With Spirits* and invite them to join the waitlist. *(N)(A)(I)*	**CLIENT GETTING ACTION:** Publish a YouTube video with **snippets of juicy content from my upcoming course.** I'll create a video titled, "3 things most mediumship mentors won't teach you." It'll have a link to my opt in in the video description and a verbal invitation to join the waitlist for my course at the end of the video as well as a link in the description. *(A)(N)(I)*	**CLIENT GETTING ACTION:** **30 Minutes engaging with my leads via email/IG/YouTube.** I'll thoughtfully answer any questions I receive via email, YT, or IG. *(N)* I'll share a resource with them like my opt in or a YouTube video that helps and also let them know I'm going deeper in my upcoming course *Speaking With Spirits* and invite them to join the waitlist. *(N)(A)(I)*
3 Elements Checklist (EER)				
Does this attempt to connect with my audience include the element of: Expertise: Y/N Resonance: Y/N Engagement: Y/N	Does this attempt to connect with my audience include the element of: Expertise: Y/N Resonance: Y/N Engagement: Y/N	Does this attempt to connect with my audience include the element of: Expertise: Y/N Resonance: Y/N Engagement: Y/N	Does this attempt to connect with my audience include the element of: Expertise: Y/N Resonance: Y/N Engagement: Y/N	Does this attempt to connect with my audience include the element of: Expertise: Y/N Resonance: Y/N Engagement: Y/N

A = Attract   *N = Nurture*   *I = Invite*

CHAPTER 9

INSPIRE

HOW TO HEAR YES FROM LEADS WITHOUT BEING PUSHY OR SLEAZY

You're spending time in the inspire category when you're taking any action in your business that inspires your followers to say yes to working with you as a paid customer. Anything you do that allows a follower to get more clarity about your offers and whether or not they're a good fit falls under the inspire part of the Client Attraction Framework. This is the step that really scares a lot of people and makes them cringe.

I get that asking for the sale can be scary. Want to know the good news? If you've really done your work on the clarity piece of the framework and you've been pulling the levers of attract, nurture, and invite, on a daily and weekly basis —and in a way that feels right for you—then the inspire part of the framework is pretty darn easy. Why? The first four pieces of the framework do all of the heavy lifting by allowing a prospect to know you, like you, and trust you. They may even wander onto your site and invest before you get the chance to make a paid offer. To give you an example of how easy the inspire part can be when you've nailed the first four steps of the Client Attraction Framework, consider that I never needed to make a sales call to sell out every single offer I made during the first 18 months of my business. That means that all of my one-on-one readings sold out, my 42 seats in my development circles either sold out, or even oversold, and nearly 50 seats in my *Speaking With Spirits* course sold without a single sales conversation. Between my free content that attracted, nurtured, and invited my audience to engage, and my sales pages that are well done and chock full of 3 P language, I didn't need to do much more than send a few sales emails and put up just a few posts on Instagram. I didn't even create sales videos on YouTube for my development circle, courses, or readings.

That being said, it's still an incredibly important part of your job to make your offers, to have a sales page or sales call when necessary, and to make it easy for your followers to sign up to become paid clients.

ALLOWING YOURSELF TO BE PAID FOR THE WORK YOU DO

If you struggle with asking for the sale, or getting paid full stop, think of the people in your life who are learning about their worth. Think about the people in your life who long to be financially empowered and are taking their cues from watching you.

When I was working as an online marketing strategist, my clients needed money to send their kids to school, to put food on the table, to buy clothes, etc. and yes, to take themselves on a vacation every now and then because earth school is hard! A lot of them were mothers and they wanted to be able to provide things for their children and for themselves. Once I became a mother myself, I thought about how my ability to earn as an entrepreneur would affect my children. I felt a sense of peace at the thought of them getting a similar example to the one that my mother gave me. My mom just went and did the stuff she wanted to do. She didn't listen to the people who told her she wasn't smart enough to get a PhD and make a living as a scientist. You bet she *was* told that but she went and did it anyway.

My girls will see that their mom has successfully run a handful of different businesses. They'll see that I earned confidence from my journey as an entrepreneur helping others. I'm hoping they'll be able to spend a lot less time questioning their right to earn and apologizing for themselves in the ways so many of my clients did when they first came to me.

I remember imagining my oldest daughter as a fine artist. In my mind I saw her showing me a piece of her artwork and sadly reporting that someone had told her that that kind of work wasn't worth anything. I imagined what I'd say. I saw myself pumping her up and talking to her about the value of art and how it enriches our lives. In my imagination, I share the story of how one of my dear friends ran a multi-six figure business teaching artists to sell portraits.

See, it's not just about you. You're an empath and I know how much you care about other people. That's why you're doing this work. You might feel guilty receiving payment, but does that solve poverty and the inequities that exist that make your heart bleed? If you don't want lots of money, great! Give your extra dollars away to people who desperately need those dollars to survive. It's sure as shit that many people with more than enough money don't have the guts to donate. Financial systems around the world are helping the rich get richer and the poor get poorer. It's not looking like they're going to change anytime soon.

If you need to, I invite you to reread chapter two. Then, make a pledge to yourself about the first step you'll take toward earning from your meaningful work.

CLIENT FEEDBACK CREATES MUST-HAVE OFFERS

We've discussed interviewing and surveying your clients. As you put your offers together, you used 3 P language to craft a great title using the title formula that I shared in chapter six.

There are two surveying best practices that I *always* use when I'm putting an offer together.

Creating Hype Survey

The first is to reach out to your followers when you're cooking up a new offer to let them know your ideas about what's coming and ask them for their feedback. This creates some good hype about your offer before it's even been formally introduced. Ultimately, you're selling before you've even made the offer by planting the seed and allowing your followers to start considering the opportunity.

For example, when creating my *Speaking With Spirits* course, I could email my subscriber list, post on social media, and even reach out personally to a few of my clients who follow me closely. In an email or post, I'd say something like this:

> *"Hey So-and-so,*
>
> *I'm so grateful you're a part of my community. I wanted to take a minute to let you know. Thank you for inspiring me to keep developing my work in ways that can help others.*
>
> *I'm also reaching out because I wondered if I could get your feedback on something I'm planning? :)*
>
> *I'm excited because I've decided to create a course. There are so many questions that students ask me in my development circle and I'm ready to create more formal training about the A-Zs of mediumship.*

If you're up for it, **would you #1) tell me the #1 thing you'd want to learn about in a mediumship course?**

Then, **#2) would you rate each of these topics on a scale of 1 - 10. 1 = not interested and 10 =** *very* **interested.**

- Creating Boundaries with Spirit
- How to Give a Mediumistic Reading
- *Connecting with Your Spirit Guides*

I only ask my clients about three topics at a time. This is so it doesn't seem like too much work for my followers to respond. The topics I choose might be topics that I'm trying to find a good title for, or that I'm wondering if my clients are truly interested in. For example, I may know that they want to know more about *How to Give a Mediumistic Reading* but maybe that title isn't as exciting as *3 Things You MUST Do Beforehand to Give an A+ Reading.* I could include both titles as topics and see which one ranks higher.

If I'm not sure if they are interested in learning *How to Connect with Your Spirit Guides* I could see how that topic is rated by them and then make the decision about whether to make it a part of my course.

Current Student Feedback Survey

The second survey is one that I send out to current students or clients to get their feedback about what they want more or less of and how they think my work with them could be even better. I use this kind of survey at the halfway point of my development circle and courses so see how things are going so far. This timing is crucial because it provides me an opportunity to make any changes that will wow my students before the course or circle has concluded. If they've given me an 8 or 9 instead of a 10/10, my plan is to make the changes they asked for prior to the end of the program so they feel like it was a 10. This is one of the best practices in my business that keeps my retention rate high. In fact, more than 50% of my clients continue to work with me over the course of multiple offers.

I use this very same survey to make sure my next upcoming offer is irresistible. After the questions in the survey about their current experience, I ask them if they are planning on investing in my next offer. I asked them why or why not. Finally, I ask them what I could add to my upcoming offer to make it an absolute no-brainer for them to say yes. To make it easier for you to implement this practice, I've listed the exact survey questions that I use below. I put these questions into a google form so that the answers can be viewed in google sheets and I can refer back to them at any time.

- Name *(I make this optional so that I get the most honest feedback possible)*
- Email *(I make this optional so that I get the most honest feedback possible)*
- How would you rate your experience in Mel's development circle so far on a scale of 1-10. 1 being poor and 10 being great.
- Is there anything you'd like more of?
- Is there anything you'd like less of?
- Do you have any suggestions so that Mel can make sure you have the best experience possible?
- What are you enjoying the most in the program?
- Please rate the community that Mel has attracted and the culture of the group that has been created for you on a scale of 1-10. 1 being poor and 10 being great. Why?
- Please rate on a scale from 1-10 your experience during class sessions. 1 being poor and 10 being great? Why?
- Are you planning to sign up for Mel's upcoming course, *Speaking With Spirits?* Why or why not?

- What would be the most exciting bonus that Mel could add to her *Speaking With Spirits* course that would make saying yes a no-brainer for you?

CRAFTING YOUR OWN SALES PAGE(S)

Depending on what your offers are, you may end up needing a sales page. I use sales pages to enroll clients in my mediumship development circle, my *Speaking With Spirits* mediumship course, and my mentorship program, *The Profitable Spiritual Medium*. I don't use longer sales pages for the readings that I offer like a spiritual assessment or a mediumship reading. For those, I simply give a description and have a purchase button.

I'm excited to share the layout that I use for a great sales page that plays a large role in converting clients into a live program or course that you might offer. The powerful thing about this sales page layout is that it effectively outlines the journey that humans take before they decide to invest in themselves through your work. Understanding this journey will help you have better conversations with prospects online, over the phone, and in person.

Reminder: creating courses and programs is a high-cost endeavor in terms of your time, money, and energy! That means that designing a sales page like this may not be necessary just yet unless you've validated your "just starting" offers and you're consistently bringing in revenue, and are ready to leverage. I recommend waiting until you've sold many of your "just starting" offers to create a longer sales page so that you are able to speak to the offer even more clearly and confidently due to your experience. If you don't feel like you've mastered the skill of speaking 3 P language with your ideal client, you might put resources of time, money, and energy into a sales page that isn't compelling and doesn't convert. Until you very much understand your ideal client's pain and pleasure points, writing sales pages takes a hell of a lot more effort unless you *are* a copywriter, or you hire one. Because I've always written my own content, I've never hired a copywriter. I'm sure I'm biased but some copywriters don't do as good of a job at truly capturing your voice—not to mention they're expensive—as entrepreneurs who figure out their 3 Ps and use them to write and speak.

I *love* this sales page layout because it takes into account how humans make decisions and it works! We've all seen hilarious infomercials, right? The step-by-step that is used on an infomercial is similar to what I'm sharing with you below, except it's not laughable and sleazy so that's always a plus. Infomercials work well because they take us on a journey that often leads to our commitment to change, becoming stronger than our fear of failure. In fact, this layout doesn't just work for a sales page. You could use it for online posts, sales videos, and sales emails.

1) Acknowledge and Understand

Focus on their pain and pleasure points here. Whatever problem, or very deep desire your client is facing, you talk about it here. First, I'll share an example infomercial style, "Are you so tired of your drains getting clogged because all of your daughters have so much hair?" Then the infomercial would elaborate on all of the painful things about drains getting clogged with hair, showing you pictures of hair everywhere in the shower and sink. For my people, it would be:

- *"Have you been through, or are you going through, a spiritual awakening?"*

- *"Do you wish you had a space to ask all of your mediumship questions and to be in community with other like-minded people?"*

- *"Do you know Spirit is calling you to this work, but you feel like one minute you're spot on and the next you feel like you're just making it all up?"*

- *"Are you ready to feel confident enough with your spiritual skills to call yourself a medium?"*

In other words, this is the section where you acknowledge, understand, and sympathize with their pain points and pleasure points.

2) Empathize and Give Hope

This is the part where you let them know that you've been there yourself. You also let them know that you've overcome the very challenges they face and achieved the outcome they desire. You share a story snippet of your journey with compelling details that show them that you know what it's like. Then you get to joyfully paint the picture of what's possible for them too. Infomercial style might sound like this, "Guess what? I have a ton of hair too, and my drain was *always* clogged, until now!" For my people, the empathy part would be:

> *"On October 25th, 2022, I had what you might call an out of body experience. It turns out that this was the beginning of my first spiritual awakening. Over the course of the following months, I had several experiences with Spirit and began giving free mediumistic readings. I experienced the roller coaster ride of emotions that comes with this work. One day, I'd give my best reading ever and I'd be over the moon when my sitter experienced the positive healing power of mediumship. The next day, I'd find myself stuck and wondering if this was really something that was possible for me. I remember*

asking myself, "When will I be able to give high quality readings consistently?" I was passionately aching to take my skills to the next level."

The giving hope part would be:

"I joined a mediumship development circle to practice giving readings regularly and enrolled in a mediumship course that could provide me with more structured learning and a space to ask every question that came to mind about mediumship.

By June of 2023, I was working professionally as a medium.

Nine months later, I had developed my own mediumship development framework that focuses on five integral aspects of mediumship development. I also began teaching by offering my own mediumship development circles.

Best of all, becoming a medium has helped me to become a better person and someone who deeply enjoys my life."

3) Clearly Present a Solution

Here's the part where you clearly present a solution that will help them overcome their pain points and experience their pleasure points. In this section, you reveal your offer, how it works, what's included, and why you believe this approach is effective. Here's the infomercial version: "Look, you can put this thingamajig in your shower drain, and you won't have hair-clogged drains anymore either!" For my people, I like to introduce the name of my live program or course and go straight into sharing my P for person.

Yup, I let them know exactly who the program is for *first*. It sounds like this:

"This live program is for you if:

- *You're just beginning your journey into the world of mediumship OR you've been practicing mediumship for some time*

- *You feel strongly pulled to mediumship and you're ready to take your Spirit skills to the next level*

- *You feel like you've gone through, or are going through, a spiritual awakening, and you're ready to deepen your understanding of how to speak with spirits*

- *You're looking for structured learning that takes you through the A-Z of what's most helpful for a medium to know while developing their craft*

- *Along with practicing your craft, you also want step-by-step education into the many aspects of mediumship development via specific training/lessons, exercises, Q&A time, and implementation sessions."*

Following that, I use 3P language to detail what they'll get. This means that everything I share with them about the program is full of language that shows them how, through my offer, they can work through their pain points and close in on their pleasure points. I then share the logistics, like how often we'll meet and where. At the end of this section, I also share the price.

4) Provide Proof

Here's where you get to build even more trust by including social proof and more story substance. You can do this by using *your* story, your clients' stories, and any testimonials that you have. Share these to show how you and others have overcome the very challenges that they're facing. Ready for the infomercial version? "These 4 families with lots of hair are now *never* worried about getting clogged drains!" My version translates into sharing as many testimonials as I have. For me, this hasn't been a problem because I collect testimonials from all of my clients who respond to my surveys—about 60%—and then use relevant testimonials on the sales page.

If I didn't have many, or any testimonials, I'd share more story snippets of my own journey that provide proof that I went through similar challenges and have overcome them.

5) Put a Cherry on Top

Here, you have an opportunity to make it easier for them to say yes. They know you understand their situation, you've shown how things have changed for you, talked about why this works and what's included, and you've shown social proof and testimonials. It's time to add in bonuses and make your offer an absolute no-brainer. The infomercial would sound just like this, "This thingamajig is just $29.99, but if you call now in the next 15 minutes, you'll get *two* thingamajigs for just $19.99!"

Here are the kind of bonuses I add:

- **BONUS #1: A Spiritual Assessment with me for the FIRST 5 who enroll.** Spiritual Assessments are intended for those who are looking for clarity and guidance regarding their intuitive and/or mediumistic skills. During a Spiritual Assessment, Mel will use the first half of your session to intuitively read into where you currently are on your spiritual path to developing as a medium or intuitive. In the second half of the assessment, Mel will work mediumistically and connect with your guides and deliver any insights, guidance, or messages to you from your spirit team.

- **BONUS #2: Small Group/Semi-Private Coaching for the FIRST 12 who enroll.** This is a 90 minute Semi-Private/Small Group Mediumship Coaching Session! These Semi-Private Coaching Sessions will include up to four mediums. Each medium will get equal time to bring questions to Mel. For the 2nd half of the coaching session, Mel will create exercises to serve the purposes and goals of the small group.

- **BONUS #3: A Cosmic Tour of the Planets, Signs and Houses: A special Astrology training about the Planets, Signs and Houses with expert Astrology So-And-So.** So-And-So will share about who the planets are, the archetypes of the signs, and the meanings of the houses. This fast-paced tour offers a basic overview of the three essential elements that form the foundation of astrology.

- **BONUS #4: $111 OFF my 12-week Mediumship Development Circle if you do BOTH!** If you decide to add on my 12 week mediumship development circle and participate in both the live course **and** circle, you'll get $111 off the investment for my circle.

The important thing about adding bonuses is making sure that they make sense when added to your main offer. The bonuses above are things that would only make my offer better for my ideal client. If I said something like, "When you enroll in my *Profitable Spiritual*

Medium mentorship program you'll get… a *new lawnmower!*" it probably wouldn't do the best job of sealing the deal.

This may also be the perfect time to add what's called a *limiter.* This is where you would extend a bonus that is only available for X amount of time, or for the first X number of people. You can see that my first two bonus offers are limiters. This adds a bit of urgency for your ideal client to go ahead and say yes if they know they want to enroll. In addition, it keeps it sustainable for you. I don't have the bandwidth to give more than five spiritual assessments and four semi-private coaching sessions as bonuses. I give paid readings and teach development circles and courses so I have to limit the number of people who get these two bonuses.

If you'd like to see examples of my sales pages, you can take a look at any of these QR codes below. Please note that all of my content is legally protected. Do not copy or plagiarize my content in any way.

THE PROFITABLE
SPIRITUAL MEDIUM

SPEAKING
WITH SPIRITS

MEDIUMSHIP
DEVELOPMENT CIRCLE

SALES EMAILS, SOCIAL POSTS, AND OUTREACH + SOCIAL PROOF

In addition to having a sales page for your medium to higher price point offers, you'll want to share these opportunities via the client attraction platforms you chose in chapter six.

You'll want to make sure that you use your list to send sales emails, that you show up on any social media platforms that you're on, *and* that you utilize personal outreach to your most engaged followers. While an outreach email should be much less formal—I'll share an example soon—your sales email and social posts can be mini versions of a sales page. For example, I'll send out a sales email to my list about my course, *Speaking With Spirits.* Then I'll create an IG video to share a lot of what I've said in the sales email. I'll also create a list of hot leads for my program and send short, two to three sentence emails saying hello, asking how they are and letting them know what I'm up to. I may not even mention my program in the first email I send.

Let's quickly recap the steps for a great sales page.

- *Acknowledge and Understand*
- *Empathize and Give Hope*
- *Clearly Present a Solution*
- *Provide Proof*
- *Put a Cherry on Top*

All I have to do for a great sales email is start with one, two, or three sentences *tops* for each of these parts. Check this out below.

Acknowledge and Understand

Ex) Do you ever feel like you have high hopes for a mediumship class or training, only to be left with the same questions? Questions like, "How do I create a stronger connection with Spirit?" "How do I trust spiritual impressions and feel more confident?"

Empathize and Give Hope

Ex) I get it. It led me to doing everything I could with my practice to answer questions like these myself. That's why I created a Mediumship Development Framework that focuses on the most important aspects of mediumship that most mediums struggle with. Things like confidence, strengthening their clairs, becoming more of a clear channel with a stronger connection to Spirit, and more! The thing is, it worked! I run my own development circle now and more than 90% of my clients rate it a 10/10!

Clearly Present a Solution

Ex) In case you're still looking for a place to practice your mediumship with a great community of like-minded people and a mentor who cares, I'd love to invite you into my Mediumship Development Circle. *(I could also go into more details about the logistics of the circle – like how many sessions, how long the sessions last, the dates, and price. etc.)*

Provide Proof

Ex) This is the part where I'd add in a testimonial. I like to intro the testimonial by saying something like, The results speak for themselves – 100% of students rated their experience 9-10/10. It's likely why my student Elizabeth said this: *"I couldn't recommend Mel's mediumship development circle more!"* – **Elizabeth.** Just in case you want to hear from her about why it's her 4th time in my circle, click HERE or on the image below. *Then I'd have a picture below of the video on my website. When they click on the picture of this video testimonial, they are brought to the part of the sales page with Elizabeth's video testimonial. If that's too techy for you, just add in a picture and a written testimonial, or a written testimonial without a picture.*

Put a Cherry on Top

> *Ex) I'm adding* **TWO juicy BONUSES for those of you who enroll!**
>
> • **Bonus #1**: *AN ENCORE Training of The Top 3 Mistakes Mediums Make when it comes to growing a business and actually making money and The EXACT 3 things to focus on INSTEAD to make a living as a medium with a 30 minute Q&A where I will answer ANY questions you ask me.*
>
> *During this training, I'll lay out my current business model, plans for expansion, and estimated revenue for this year!*
>
> • **Bonus #2**: *Design Your 90-Day Business Profit Plan (Training and Workshop for Mediums).*
>
> *I'll also be gifting you a powerful 90-minute training and workshop to help you design your 90-Day Profit Plan as a medium! There's no reason you can't make back the investment for this Mediumship Development Circle over a 90-day period if you implement what you'll learn in this training.*

If I wanted to create a social post, I'd just shorten it up a bit more. See how I do it below.

Acknowledge and Understand

> *Ex)* Do you ever feel like you have high hopes for a mediumship class or training, only to be left feeling like you haven't improved much?

Empathize and Give Hope

Ex) I get it. It's why I created a Mediumship Development Framework that focuses on the most important aspects of mediumship that most mediums struggle with. I run my own development circle now and more than 90% of my clients rate my circle a 10/10!

Clearly Present a Solution

Ex) In case you're still looking for a place to practice your mediumship, I'd love to invite you into my Mediumship Development Circle.

Provide Proof

Ex) This is the part where I'd add in a testimonial. I like to introduce the testimonial by saying something like, The results speak for themselves: 100% of students rate their experience 9-10/10. It's my client Elizabeth's 4th time in my circle!

Put a Cherry on Top

Ex) I'm adding **TWO juicy BONUSES for those of you who enroll!**
- **Bonus #1**: *AN ENCORE Training of The Top 3 Mistakes Mediums Make when it comes to growing a business and actually making money and*
- **Bonus #2:** *Design Your 90-Day Business Profit Plan (Training and Workshop for Mediums)*

For a social post, I could also just share the testimonial and development circle invite, telling people why Elizabeth has taken my circle four times and then sharing a link. You don't *always* need all five elements in every sales email or social post, but you do need to always provide a solution and social proof.

In terms of client outreach to an engaged follower, I do something that is a lot less formal and short and sweet. I wrote this outreach email to a client who had done a one-on-one spiritual assessment reading with me. I followed up with her after the assessment and let her know I enjoyed working with her. We'd had a little back and forth before I sent this email. When my development circle opened for enrollment, I thought of her and emailed her this:

> Hey Sandi,
>
> How are you? It was such a pleasure to give you a Spiritual Assessment back in August!
>
> I'm reaching out to see if you have given any thought to joining my Mediumship Development Circle?
>
> After diving into your spiritual development with you during your reading, I've been thinking about this opportunity for you. I have two seats left that I just added in my Wednesday evening circle.
>
> No pressure whatsoever, but I'd love to hear how you're doing and your thoughts!
>
> Lots of love,
>
> Mel

Social Proof

What is social proof and why is it important? Social proof is seeing examples of other people who are in a similar situation to you, having the success that you desire. For example, you're reading this book because you're a spiritual practitioner, likely a medium, and you want to create a profitable 6-figure and beyond business. You see that I've done it myself. If you look on my sales page using the QR code, you'll see that I have clients who have also done it with my help through my *Profitable Spiritual Medium* mentorship program.

You can probably tell why social proof is a must, right? When you want something badly, but it takes the resources of time, money, and energy to make it happen, a lot of us feel like we want some kind of evidence that our desire is possible. We want to know that other people have succeeded. We want to know how they did it. This makes it more real for us. It makes us more willing to invest our resources to create the result.

I'm always adding new testimonials to my services page and to the sales pages for my courses. I want to show that my offers work. I've invested many times because I wanted to create something and had all of the nerves about taking that next step. Saying yes becomes less of an anxiety-provoking choice for your followers when there's social proof. The more you can capture the success stories of your students and get permission to share about their experience with prospective clients, the better. Make it a habit and an automated practice in your business and you won't be sorry!

HAVING NON-SLEEZY SALES CONVERSATIONS

I'm honored and excited to help you invite your leads to say yes to working with you. That being said, sales conversations, like a sales page, will not always be necessary. I don't do sales calls for private readings, group readings, my development circle, or my *Speaking With Spirits* course. However, as my offers become higher-priced,

I will open up time to speak to people who have questions before enrolling.

Sales conversations have gotten a bad rap, but they should be high-integrity, honest, and transparent. They're about creating space for the potential client to sort out their decision with your support. There's no one right way to lead your potential client through a sales call. The structure I'm teaching you is what I find works best for me and many of my clients. If you discover a different way, great. Let learning this approach serve its purpose by helping you create a foundation that you can tweak if need be.

I won't be giving you a script. Instead, I'll be providing you with a structure that I personally think kicks buns. It's a compilation of things I've learned over my time studying and practicing sales for the past 17+ years. With this structure, you'll know exactly where to guide the conversation. There's also room for you to design your own questions that feel genuine to you and the type of support you provide.

This structure is provided to create freedom. Be wary of creating a script so tight that it takes you out of the present moment with your potential client. If you are truly listening to the human you're speaking with, the next question will come to you because it will make logical sense to ask it. As you come to know and understand that the goal of the conversation is to help your potential client find clarity, that will help guide your conversation too. Ultimately, you will have enough structure to lean back and let the conversation naturally flow, while still being conscious of where it's going and how to ask powerful questions that keep it on track.

Getting Your Mind in the Game Before the Call

The time just before a sales conversation, or even during it, can be a little nerve-racking. I remember getting so nervous beforehand—even though I had been over the moon to have someone book a call to talk about my course or program—that I would sit hoping that the potential client would cancel. As soon as I began the conversation though, I always felt better.

Here are a couple of tools I used to prepare myself for the call:

1) I create reminders that resonate and I repeat them to myself before I get on the phone.

Here are some reminders I created that helped calm me and keep me grounded.

- *"There are more than enough clients out there for me. For every potential client I speak with, there are three more waiting to say yes."*
- *"My only intention is to truly discover if it is a good fit for the two of us to work together by staying open, present, and being curious. I promise myself that I will ask every question that I know to ask before getting off the phone if there's room for more inquiry."*
- *"No matter the outcome of this call, there are unlimited ways for me to create the outcome I desire, and in the timing that is right."*

Can you think of any reminders that you'd like to say out loud or adopt?

2) I remind myself that this time is very much about them.

Yes, I'm making sure that the potential client is a good fit for me. But putting the focus on them and how they must be feeling really helps. People are coming to us because they are struggling to change or have an experience and feel they need help. They most likely *want* you to be the person to have the right support for them. Practice putting yourself in their shoes to stop yourself from making this time about you and your fears.

Structuring Your Sales Conversations

1) Opening the Conversation and Getting on the Same Page

Most comfortable conversations start out with a warm welcome so your ideal clients know you're genuinely excited to connect with them. Then it's important to communicate clearly with them about the purpose of the call.

Here's what this looks like in terms of opening the conversation:

> *"Hey [name of prospect] thank you for spending your time with me today. I'm excited to get to know you. I understand you're interested in possibly working with me in my [insert name of offer], is that true?"*

They usually say yes. They might also say something like, *"Well, I want to hear more about your program…"*

Either way, I say, *"Great! The purpose of this call is to see if working together is something that could benefit you, and if it's a good fit. Does that sound ok to you?"* 99.9% of the time they say yes, which is great, because now you're both on the same page and that takes a lot of the pressure off.

If for any reason you get a no to the first question or a response, that lets you know that this potential client is not currently ready to discuss working with you at this time. Still, you can politely and warmly let them know that any details they'd like about your work and packages are on your website. Feel free to share any of your free content that you think would be beneficial to them or invite them to your next free training. Let them know that you'd love to have this sales conversation at a later time, when and if they are interested in potentially working with you. Don't be afraid to stand up for your boundaries. You can offer free content, give opportunities for potential clients to sample your work, and/or do pro bono coaching as often as you'd like. Sales conversations have a specific purpose though. That purpose is to find clarity on whether or not working together via a paid offer is the right fit for them.

What feels most authentic to you in terms of opening the conversation and getting on the same page as your ideal client? Think about the way you like to welcome someone to a conversation so that they feel comfortable. How would you like to make sure you're on the right page from the start?

2) Where are they, where do they want to be, and why?

After you've opened the conversation and gotten on the same page with your potential client about the purpose of the call, you can begin asking questions about where they are, where they would like to be, and why. The more you understand their values and what motivates them, the better you'll be able to speak their language. Many times, entrepreneurs hear "no" because they don't know how to speak to the motivations that underlie everything else that is discussed during the sales conversation. The problem is that without digging deeper, you can't help the potential client bring forth their vision to a level that helps them overcome any hesitations and fears.

Lead with curiosity. Take your time. Don't rush when it comes to understanding who they are and what they need. Before you can really support them, give advice, or make your offer, you need to know the details of their current circumstance and what they're looking to create. What pieces do they already have in place when it comes to solving their puzzle? What, if any, support have they had previously? How was that experience? What worked for them and what didn't work for them? Where would they like to see themselves in the next six months? What are they specifically looking to get from your support? I dig deep here. If they say things that I'm curious about like *"Yeah, that previous hire/support didn't work for me..."* I definitely ask, *"What about it didn't work for you?"* I mirror their exact language and get clear on what's going on, plus why it's unfolded in the way that it has.

Some questions I like to ask during this part of the conversation are:

"What's your vision in terms of (their P for pleasure)?"

"What would you want to get out of our work together?"

"Why is this so important to you?"

"How are you thinking things would change if you created x, y, z?"

Think about the things that you really need to know about someone before committing to support them. The more present you are in the conversation, the better you'll be at asking questions that flow and go deeper into their story. Additionally, if there's a question you want to ask that feels like it might be somewhat private, but you'd really like to know the answer and you feel it would serve the purpose of the call, ask permission first.

Think now about what questions would feel genuine to you in order to understand your client's current situation, where they'd like to be instead, and why.

3) What are their challenges?

It's important that you understand their unique challenges. This can be tricky if your client likes to minimize or hide their struggles.

Remember that these challenges are the reason they're coming to you. We're not focusing on their challenges or pain points so that we can make them squirt tears. For a human to change and have the motivation to do what it takes, they've got to be aware of what isn't working. This helps them realize what will need to shift in order to get a better result.

As obvious as it may seem when it's not you, humans slip into the trap of not realizing that they're acting like a hamster on a wheel. The fact that they're working their buns off and sometimes making little or even no progress can be a blindspot for them. To have their situation reflected back can be very eye opening.

When you help your client reveal the reasons for the gap between where they are and where they want to be, you're helping them get clarity on whether or not they're available to continue on in this way. You're also allowing them to become aware of the support you feel they need. If you can provide that support, then huzzah! It's a great fit! If not, you can refer them elsewhere. This part of the conversation is a powerful way to help people make decisions that move them forward, whether it means working with you or not.

Some of the questions I ask are:

> *"What challenges are you facing?"*
> *"What's keeping you from getting x, y, z result?"*
> *"What have you tried that hasn't worked?"*

Be curious. What questions will you ask to uncover the challenges that your potential client is facing?

4) Is this a now thing?

Most people who make significant changes have a sense of urgency in accomplishing their desires. When I say urgency, I don't mean being frenzied. They aren't necessarily running around in an absolute tizzy. Simply put, the humans who get results are ready to take action.

Some of the questions I ask are:

"Is it important for you to transform this now?"

"Why do you desire to solve this problem now instead of six months from now?"

"Are you looking to invest time, money, and energy in this now?"

"What do you imagine will happen if you don't take action now?"

"Where do you imagine you will be in 3-6 months if you don't put the time in now?

"What does this mean to you? How does this feel to you?"

What questions would you ask to reveal your client's sense of urgency?

5) How dedicated are they?

Helping your potential client discover how dedicated they are is a must in my book. Just like having a sense of urgency gets the best results, being dedicated and persistent is what it takes for most people to achieve something they are passionate about. I see people every day who feel compelled by their desires. What I don't see every day are humans who have the dedication and commitment to keep showing up. This is because change is not easy. The human you're speaking with is coming to you because they haven't been able to get the result they want on their own. Potential clients find clarity and conviction within themselves when you open up space for them to talk through this aspect.

Here are some questions I love to use:

"How dedicated are you to transforming x, y, z?"

"Do you feel willing to put the work in to achieve x, y, z outcome?"

"Is there anything that you think you'll need to change about yourself and/or your circumstance in order to have the outcome you want?"

"How committed are you to getting support to go to the next level?"

Think about the questions you will ask to reveal how dedicated your potential client is.

6) Recap and make sure they feel heard.

This part of the conversation can be validating for your ideal client. How often do people feel that they are truly listened to? Your potential client needs to feel like you see where they're coming from. They want to be understood and to know that you "get them."

Recap what you've heard them say by summing up the conversation so far. Use their exact words as you repeat back to them their story and situation. If they say they're nervous to develop their spiritual skills, don't say they're *scared* to develop their spiritual skills. Use the word nervous. This ensures that you're mirroring their situation in a way that sounds true for them. Knowing that they are heard and understood creates trust and allows them to see that you are the right person to help them go from where they are, to where they want to be.

After you summarize what you're hearing, ask them if what you've stated sounds true to them. They'll say yes if you've done a good job of listening and using their words. Finally, ask if there is anything else that:

- you've left out
- that they would like you to add
- that they feel is significant for you to know

Once they feel heard, ask them the following:

> *"Based on what you're telling me, if you were to have [the support that they need and you offer], do you believe that you could create [the result that they desire to create]?"*

This question helps them to get clear on whether it's the right thing to consider working with you.

Do you think you'll use this question? Do you desire to frame it differently? What words resonate with you to help the client see how they might transform with your support?

7) Share with them what working together looks like.

At this point in the conversation I say:

> *"Is it ok with you if I let you know what your role would be in creating success for yourself, who I am as a coach/ mentor/facilitator, and exactly what we'll dive into together as we begin our work?"*

This is where the benefit laden phrases from chapter six that convey the value of your work come in. The *So That You Can* bullet formula is helpful here. You'll use these phrases according to the needs of the client. Remember to use their words too. We want them to understand the benefit of our work and how it applies to the results they are passionate about creating for themselves.

1) What their role is in order to create success

This is about managing clients' expectations with honesty and integrity about what it will take to develop their skills and/or get the results. Whatever comes up for you about the actions they'll need to take or the changes they might need to make, create clear language around it that you can present to your ideal client so they understand what will be expected of them.

2) Who you are as a mentor

This is about informing the client about what they can expect from you. I let my clients know that I will show up 100% as their coach/mentor/facilitator. It's also great to let them know how you work and what your style is. I share that I love to laugh and use humor, but that I expect them to perform at their highest level.

3) What beginning your work together will look like

This is your chance to unleash those sexy phrases that you've put together. Pinpoint three main tools/areas of focus that you'll be diving into with them in order to have a simple and effective plan to help them create their x, y, z desire.

How will you explain what working together will look like in a way that shows the value of what you do? Let's say that my client wanted to develop their clairaudience, have a stronger connection to Spirit, and feel more confident as a medium. First, remember this tool:

I'll help you _____ so that you can _____ and _____.
        (Tool)   (Pleasure)   (Pleasure)

Below is an example of the three 3P phrases that I might use after listening to their goals.

- I'll teach you my two favorite ways to develop clairaudience through meditation and music, so that you can start accurately bringing through jaw-dropping evidence clairaudiently.
- I'll help you learn how to become a clear channel for Spirit so that your readings become more consistently accurate and you feel confident that you're connected to Spirit.
- I'll help you learn to be unphased by hearing *no* from your sitter so that you become confident and proud to call yourself a medium.

Can you see how this is a powerful way to let your potential client know what's possible? You're directly addressing their biggest pain and pleasure points. Do you understand how this language effectively paints the picture of the power of working with you?

8) Let them tell you why it feels like a great fit (if it does).

After you've clearly explained what working with you looks like, check in to make sure that your help is what they're looking for. These questions let your potential client tell *you* why working with you is a good fit.

Some of the questions I ask at this point are:

"How does that sound?"

If they say, "I love it!" I would ask, "What do you love about it?"

"What do you see yourself getting during our work together?"

"Does this program feel like a great fit to you? What about it feels like a great fit?"

"Why do you feel I might be the right coach for you?

What questions will you ask to let them tell you why working together feels right?

9) Presenting program details and asking for the sale and helping your client sign up.

I put my offers and prices on my website. If a potential client feels like I'm the right mentor for them, I share all of the logistical details of my offer before we chat.

I usually say something like this:

"The program/course/offer that would serve you best is my x, y, z ..."

You can remind them of the features and details of your offer, plus any bonuses. Continue to mix in your benefit laden phrases that convey the value you provide. Just keep the pitch short and succinct. Overwhelming them with information can confuse your prospect and may lead to hesitations. This is because the confused customer never invests.

Once you've shared the details and any bonuses, state the pay in full price. If they inquire about payment plans, absolutely share. Keep it as simple and as easy to understand as possible.

Once I state my price, I ask them, "Would you like to get started?" Then I give them the time and space to respond. It's ok and normal to allow some silence. If you get nervous and start defending your price or trying to fill up the moment with words, it can erode your prospect's confidence in you and may appear as if you're attempting to justify your price. Be confident in your offer. Take your time and give them space to process.

When they say YES, congratulate and welcome them!

At this point, you can get them signed up in a few different ways:

1. You can let them know what they'll receive once they register, and enroll them right there over the phone or in person.
2. You can direct them to a link to register online, and stay with them on the phone as they register. Let them know you'd like to be there to welcome them.
3. You can send them the link in an email and tell them to register by a certain date and time.

10) Following up

If you don't get a full yes on the phone

If your potential client hasn't said yes for any other reason, do your best to schedule a follow up time to chat again. I suggest scheduling the follow up call within a few days or a week tops. If they have something they need to do, like go to the bank, or check in with a spouse, that's when you can say something like, *"Great! When do you plan on x, y, z-ing?"* Then, *"Wonderful, are you available to jump back on the phone on X date at Y time and I can support you on any necessary next steps?"*

You've done the hard work, built the trust, and they're excited. Continuing the conversation soon after is important. Investments are significant and it's easy for a potential client to fall into fear or doubt themselves. That's why they need your support. You can help them change their life by keeping the faith, instead of getting stuck in fear and staying in the exact same place.

If It's a No or Not Yet

How long I wait to follow up varies. Sometimes clients tell me specific dates or times that they feel will be right for us to begin working together. Other times they don't mention anything.

Following up multiple times is a good thing to do. Stats show that as many as 14 touch points are appropriate. Do what feels best to you. On average, I follow up once a month. If for any reason you feel inclined to follow up sooner, follow your intuition. Definitely steer clear of reaching out with an annoying message like, "Ready to get started?!" Instead, send a very short and sweet note, so that they'll actually read it, and say something like,

> *"Was thinking of you and wondered how you're doing! Would love an update. How are things with your x, y, z situation?"*

IDENTIFYING YOUR DIFFERENTIATOR

What is a differentiator? It's something that is unique and different about the way that you work. It helps you stand out from others who may have similar offers for the same target market. Identifying your differentiator is not something you have to know today, but here are some ways that you can think about a distinctive aspect of your work that might help you stand out in a sea of spiritual entrepreneurs:

- Specializing in something specific within your area of focus
  - Examples of this might be that you focus primarily on animal communication, assist law enforcement to help solve crimes, or work with those who are nearing transition.
- Working with a specific group or niche of people

- Examples of this might be that you focus primarily on pet owners, work with parents who are grieving a child, or help families who have lost a loved one to suicide.
- A certain modality or method that you use to help your clients get results
  - Examples of this might be that you do energy work along with your readings, use props like crystals, tea leaves, scrying, cards, etc. or a teaching style that works well with your ideal clients.

What seems like a tiny detail can make all of the difference when it comes to becoming known for something and getting your name out there to attract clients consistently. Over 50% of my students tell me that they choose to work with me because they love my structured and step-by-step teaching style. It might seem like a minute detail, but the fact that I have a framework for the way I teach and step-by-step mediumship hacks makes me very different from other mediumship mentors.

If you don't recognize a differentiator for yourself right now, don't sweat it. As you work with more clients, a certain target market, modality that you use, or area of focus may pop out at you. Something else that's really helpful in this case? Look back at the list of tools you created and see if your differentiator may be obvious. It could be an overarching step that makes up your CRF or CEF.

When I was an online marketing strategist, my differentiator was one of my overarching steps within my CRF. It was my fifth step, inspire. I was the mentor that people came to when they wanted help with their sales process. I had a sales course and a free sales assessment, both named *Master Your Money Conversations*. Remember that my best free content was *The Top 10 Ways To Book 20+ Sales Calls A Month*. The extra detail that I put into creating sales content was what set me apart from other business coaches. Voila, it made it a no-brainer for my ideal audience members to choose me over someone who didn't specialize in sales.

The important thing about identifying your differentiator is that it should be congruent with the work that you do and the needs of your audience. Just because you're a talented website designer, for example, doesn't mean that your mediumship clients will come to you because of that. Website design *clearly* isn't something directly related to giving readings and teaching mediumship. Pickin' up what I'm puttin' down?

If you're going to identify a specialty as your differentiator, make sure that it's a tool that is desired by your ideal client and an obvious help in getting them what they're coming to you for. If you're going to target a certain group of people, make sure that they're a population that greatly needs and desires the kind of support and service that you provide. If you're going to identify a method or modality, make sure that it's obvious to your target that this method or modality is a significant part of helping them get what they want – maybe even in a way no other method or modality ever has. If you have some thoughts or ideas about what yours might be, write them down now. If you don't, head back to your framework and see if it gives you some clues. Don't worry if you still come up dry. A differentiator is something that can't be forced but that naturally develops over time as you evolve your craft.

CONCLUSION

From the very bottom of my heart, thank you so very much for picking up this book. The fact that you're reading this now means you *do* have the courage to make a living as a medium. Your work with Spirit has called you to take your skills to a professional level. I know this because I have *never* had someone come to me with the desire to make a living as a medium who wasn't meant for it. People like my husband, I love him dearly and he's the best man I know, are *not* meant for this work. They don't feel the pull. You do.

You have confidence that there's value in the work that you provide. You've given readings and been thanked afterward for the life-changing experience. Now you can put words to that experience, and with confidence, because you're speaking to the 3 Ps of your absolute ideal client!

You have expertise to offer to help your clients experience something wonderful, and perhaps create skills or an outcome that they've been hoping for. You've got your CRF and your CEF mapped out so you're aware of the process you use that's uniquely you and gets results.

You've designed a Client Pathway Pyramid that's downright brilliant because your followers can hike right on up that pyramid and be supported by you and your offers on their journey. You've created must-have, drool-worthy, free content that is so perfectly suited for them that they're peeing their pants to get a hold of it!

You know how to spend your time in a way that will put you on the path to success and profitability. While your other medium friends are suckers who are pulling their hair out over their website, you know how to pull the levers of attract, nurture, and invite in a fraction of the time that it takes others to struggle over what to put on their silly home page. Be a pal. Give them this book to put them out of their misery – and I *don't* mean kill them – and onto the fast track.

It's all a pretty big fuckin' deal and now it's time for the rubber to meet the road if it hasn't already! In my usual Mel fashion: here's your game-plan. If you don't yet have clarity about your 3 Ps, offer, and the price, now is the time. It doesn't need to be perfect. Just make some choices. You can always make changes as you move forward.

Next, pull the levers of attract, nurture, and invite five days a week. Remember that pulling these three levers doesn't have to mean that you're taking colossal actions each and every day. You might send a single email to someone you keep thinking about for your development circle. Maybe you share an insight you got from Spirit that you feel will be moving and helpful to your audience via a short video reel. Take steps each day, even if they're small.

Sprinkle in the inspire aspect of the framework when you're ready to make your offer, or simply watch readings get booked straight off your website. I made a promise to myself that if I did nothing else, I would take actions that fall within the five part framework each day of the week. It worked for me, and it will work for you.

If you haven't given yourself permission to receive money for the incredible work that you do, then I'm giving it to you now. People all over the world are earning a living doing every kind of job. It's your turn to be compensated for the good you contribute to this world as a medium and to allow abundance to come to you. I know how long you've been waiting to call yourself a professional medium and how scary it can feel when you take the plunge. Just promise me this: if you're still shaking in your boots, know that you can be scared *and* take the next step. What you choose teaches the people around you that they have permission to either hide in fear or step up to the challenge and fulfill their purpose and life's work. That's the responsibility that comes with the freedom to do this work, that by the way, you're privileged to have. You're not at earth school by accident, so get to it, won't you? In the words of one of my favorite activists on this planet, "Pressure is a privilege." Thanks Billie Jean King.

I gave a reading to a grandmother and granddaughter one day. The grandmother was full of life, not someone who had avoided hardship, but who had chosen to find joy in the life she was still living. The granddaughter looked as if the light in her eyes was dull and drained of color. As I warmly welcomed them both, I couldn't help but feel the energetic brick wall that this young woman had fortified around herself. It was a defense mechanism no doubt and a response to the sheer heartbreak and pain that she was experiencing. I knew instantly that her mother was waiting to speak to them both.

As her mother offered apologies for the pain she had caused when she was living, her daughter kept a stone face. Tears slid down her cheeks and she quickly wiped them away. She looked away from me much of the time. I looked away too, simply to offer her the privacy she deserved. She didn't say much, but at the end of the reading she looked into my eyes and thanked me. There was a little more life in her eyes and a little less anger.

After the reading, I got an email from the grandmother. She said she'd been signing up for large group readings for *years* and never been able to hear from her passed daughter. Our reading that day had finally been what she had been hoping for, and what she believed her granddaughter really needed, even if she hadn't said as much.

There's someone out there right now who's been searching for the kind of reading only you can give, to connect them with their passed loved one(s). I know you have the courage, and now you have the know-how.

If you get stuck, just know that I'm only an email or YouTube channel away. This isn't where our journey ends. If you know you want me to hold your hand through this entire process, you can jump on the waitlist for my mentorship program, *The Profitable Spiritual Medium* using the QR code. If you just want to keep connecting, you can follow me online on YouTube or Instagram @mediumshipwithmel. Here's to your future as a profitable spiritual medium!

WORKS REFERENCED

https://www.ziprecruiter.com/Salaries/Psychic-Medium-Salary

https://www.ziprecruiter.com/Salaries/What-Is-the-Average-Psychic-Mediu
m-Salary-by-State

https://iwpr.org/national-gender-wage-gap-widens-significantl
y-in-2023-for-the-first-time-in-20-years/

https://www.pewresearch.org/short-reads/2025/03/04/gender-pay-gap-in-us-ha
s-narrowed-slightly-over-2-decades/

https://www.equalpaytoday.org/gender-pay-gap-statistics/

https://www.cnbc.com/2025/03/25/equal-pay-day-highlights-stalled-progres
s-on-closing-gender-pay-gap.html

https://www.fidelitycharitable.org/articles/
giving-similarities-outweigh-differences-men-women-entrepreneurs.html

ACKNOWLEDGMENTS

When I share that I wrote two books, created two courses, and birthed my second daughter all in one year, I suppose it sounds impressive. The truth is that the love and support that surrounds me from my family and friends is unparalleled. Aubyn, once again, as my editor, you have pulled the best out of me. Each time I thought I was done I'd get an email notification from the google doc of my manuscript saying, "You're better than this." I'll see you again soon with my next book. Sara, you've created an environment, a community, and a belief system within so many other humans that convinces us we can do something like write a book. Thank Spirit for you. Emily, our conversation in Essex at the pub where I helped you map out some marketing plans was a pivotal moment for me. You are a true friend and a wonderful person, full stop. Thank Spirit that we met at AFC and that you aggressively pursued our friendship. It has been one of the best gifts *ever*. Mom, with every passing year I seem to become more aware of the many gifts you've given me. Growing up, I've had the chance to witness you earn your degrees, teach students with exhilarating joy, and lead and create your legacy that focused on making education more accessible for marginalized groups. In so many ways you have inspired me to hold fast to my ideals, even in a world where so many stop believing in miracles. Rob, thank you for your beautiful expression of unconditional love. Being with you makes me better and your support and true partnership is a large part of what has made this book possible. To everyone not named, but who has contributed simply by loving me and believing in me, I'm grateful.

ABOUT THE AUTHOR

Photo cred Wendy Yalom Photography

Melissa Pharr is a professional spiritual medium, mom, wife, and businesswoman. She didn't pop out seeing dead people as a kid (at least not that she can remember) and never imagined running a business as a spiritual practitioner. She now sells out mediumship development circles, mediumship readings, and courses of all kinds, bringing peace and closure to those who sit with her and a down-to-earth and straightforward approach to mediumship for aspiring mediums. Mel has studied residentially at the Arthur Findlay College in Essex, UK, and continues her studies via tutors, mediumship development circles, and trainings with the Arthur Findlay College and the Journey Within Spiritualist Church.

www.ingramcontent.com/pod-product-compliance
Lightning Source LLC
Chambersburg PA
CBHW051301120626
46547CB00015B/2042